Silence Is Not Golden

Silence Is Not Golden

Strategies for Helping the Shy Child

Christopher A. Kearney

OXFORD
UNIVERSITY PRESS
2011

OXFORD
UNIVERSITY PRESS

Oxford University Press, Inc., publishes works that further
Oxford University's objective of excellence
in research, scholarship, and education.

Oxford   New York
Auckland   Cape Town   Dar es Salaam   Hong Kong   Karachi
Kuala Lumpur   Madrid   Melbourne   Mexico City   Nairobi
New Delhi   Shanghai   Taipei   Toronto

With offices in
Argentina   Austria   Brazil   Chile   Czech Republic   France   Greece
Guatemala   Hungary   Italy   Japan   Poland   Portugal   Singapore
South Korea   Switzerland   Thailand   Turkey   Ukraine   Vietnam

Published by Oxford University Press, Inc.
198 Madison Avenue, New York, New York 10016
www.oup.com

Oxford is a registered trademark of Oxford University Press

Library of Congress Cataloging-in-Publication Data

Kearney, Christopher A.
  Silence is not golden : strategies for helping the shy child / Christopher A. Kearney.
     p. cm.
  ISBN 978-0-19-532662-8 (pbk.)
  1. Bashfulness in children. 2. Child rearing. I. Title.
  BF723.B3K43 2011
  649'.64--dc22   2010008772

1 3 5 7 9 8 6 4 2
Printed in the United States of America
on acid-free paper

Contents

1

Defining Shyness

"Samantha always seems so shy and will not approach people at school. I feel worried for her. What can I do?"

"Evan cries a lot and just seems so unhappy around other children. This is so stressful for all of us. How can we help our son?"

"The school just told me that Jaden will not talk to anyone at school. Why is she doing this? What will happen to her?"

"Ryan just seems to mope around a lot and never wants to play with friends. He even wants us to place him in home schooling. I'm so confused. Should I teach him at home?"

"Isabel complains of headaches and stomachaches around people and always wants to leave birthday parties and other social events early. What can we do to make life easier for her?"

"Tashi just moved here and seems so shy. I thought she would have gotten over her initial fears by now. What can I do to help her?"

Do any of these situations sound familiar to you? When a child is overly shy or seems unhappy around other people, family members are often frustrated, distressed, concerned, and confused. But that's understandable. After all, we naturally expect our children to have friends, associate with others, and enjoy social interactions. If your child has trouble relating to others or will not even speak to others, then you might be wondering: What do I do? What might happen? How can I get my child more interested in social situations? All of these reactions are perfectly normal.

Having a child who is overly shy and who has trouble interacting with others can be upsetting because we do not like our children to be distressed and we worry what will happen if they do not have friends. What makes intense shyness even more upsetting is that the behavior can be hard to understand. But be assured—you *can* get your overly shy child to develop friendships and have a good quality of life. The main purpose of this book is to help you understand the different parts of shyness and to give you and your child the means to handle these different parts. The main purpose of this chapter is to explain shyness and to give you an idea of what this book is about.

What Is Shyness and Social Situations?

All of us act with different levels of nervousness in social situations (see Fig. 1.1). Some people seem fearless when they meet someone new or speak before others—we often admire this quality in a person! Most of us, though, are somewhat nervous when we meet someone for the first time or when we go on a job interview or blind date. This is normal. Our nervousness in these situations usually eases once we get accustomed to the person or situation and once our confidence grows.

Other people are a bit higher on the spectrum of social discomfort and are shy (Fig. 1.1). All of us have a pretty good idea of what shyness is—we seem to know it when we see it—but shyness does have different parts. Shyness generally refers to the following:

- Possible physical discomfort around others
- Concerns or worry about evaluations from others
- A tendency to withdraw from social situations and pursue solitary activities

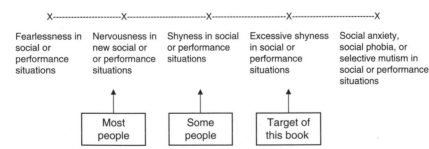

Figure 1.1. Spectrum of social discomfort.

Many people are shy! Researchers estimate that 20–48% of the general population is shy. Shyness is a kind of temperament or emotional state or personality trait that many people have. Shyness itself is normal and is not necessarily a bad thing. *Excessive shyness*, however, can be a problem and is the focus of this book (Fig. 1.1).

Social situations refer to settings in which we interact with others or perform before others. Children interact with other children and adults in many situations such as school, church, recreational centers, extra-curricular activities, sporting events, and gatherings like sleepovers, parties, or family reunions. Children also perform before others in situations that involve academic, athletic, musical, or other feats. Examples include tests, physical education class, writing on a blackboard, recitals, and oral presentations. Many shy children can navigate these social and performance situations but some cannot. Overly shy children often have problems with the following situations as well:

- Answering or talking on the telephone
- Asking others such as teachers for help
- Changing for physical education class
- Inviting others to play
- Ordering food in a restaurant or eating in public places
- Participating in group or team meetings
- Reading before others or answering questions in class
- Starting or maintaining a conversation
- Using school or public restrooms
- Walking in hallways at school or eating in the school cafeteria
- Working with others on group projects

Think for a moment about your overly shy child. Does she have trouble in these situations? Are there other situations or settings in which she has difficulty? Other situations will be covered in Chapter 2. Some shy children seem fine in some situations, especially familiar ones, but do less well in new or unfamiliar surroundings. Shy children also show different symptoms or behaviors, as described in more detail below.

The Parts of Shyness

Shyness has different parts, so let's examine each part in detail. Some people who are overly shy have *physical discomfort* when around other people, especially people they do not know well. Recall that Isabel has headaches and stomachaches around other people. Not all shy people have physical discomfort around other people, but some do. Possible physical symptoms in overly shy children, especially when around others, include the following:

- Blushing
- Breathlessness or hyperventilation
- Dizziness
- Frequent urination or diarrhea
- Headaches and stomachaches
- Increased heart rate
- Muscle tension
- Nausea or vomiting
- Sweating
- Trembling and shaking

Keep in mind that many overly shy children do not have any physical symptoms. Your overly shy child may also have physical symptoms that are not on this list, and that is okay. Keep in mind as well that some physical nervousness is normal in many situations. Think about attending a job interview, speaking before others, or going on a blind date. All of these situations create some physical change such as increased heart rate, but most of us can control these changes or see that they ease over time. Other people have more difficulty controlling these physical symptoms.

Another part of shyness is *worrisome thoughts* a person has in social situations. Recall that overly shy people sometimes have concerns or worry about evaluations from others. Some shy people are quite anxious about what other people think of them and *worry they will be embarrassed or humiliated.* Shy people sometimes have other thoughts or concerns as well:

- Appearing foolish or nervous before others
- Being excluded from a social group
- Being ignored by others when speaking or asking for help
- Being incompetent or inadequate in a social or other way
- Being scared or harmed in some way in social situations
- Blushing
- Lack of friends and feelings of isolation from others.
- Negative evaluation or ridicule from other people
- Trouble concentrating

A third part of shyness involves *actual behavior* such as a tendency to withdraw from others or to pursue solitary activities. Many children that are overly shy, like Samantha, do not approach other children or invite them to play. Other shy children want to participate *only* in solitary activities such as playing the piano or playing by themselves. Shy children sometimes do the following:

- Avoid or escape from social situations
- Cry, throw temper tantrums, or cling to adults in social situations
- Display a shaky voice or "freeze" in social situations
- Seek frequent reassurance from others such as parents
- Show odd rituals such as twirling or shaking in social situations
- Show poor eye contact or other social skills when speaking to others

Again, the main parts of shyness are (1) possible physical symptoms, (2) worrisome thoughts about embarrassment or incompetence in social situations, and (3) actual behaviors such as withdrawal, avoiding social situations, or pursuing solitary activities. Some shy children show all three parts and some just show one or two parts—each child is different. Think about your shy child—does he mostly show physical symptoms, worrisome thoughts, avoidance behaviors, or some combination?

Types of Shyness

You may have heard other words sometimes used to describe people who are shy. The following are some different phrases related to shyness:

- *Inhibition* refers to fearfulness, timidity, avoidance, and guardedness about new situations or people.
- *Introversion* refers to a quiet and reserved nature or preference to be alone.
- *Private shyness* refers to people who have good social skills—such as eye contact and the ability to maintain a conversation—but much self-doubt.
- *Public shyness* refers to people who do not have good social skills and are very distressed in social situations.
- *Self-consciousness* refers to embarrassment from feeling that others are aware of you and are being critical of you.
- *Social withdrawal* refers to little contact with peers compared to most children of that age.

You can see there are different kinds of shyness-related types. Do any of these seem to apply to your child? If you do not see a clear type for your child, that is okay. Many children do not show a specific type of shyness or they show more than one type in different situations. A child may show good social skills but intense self-doubt in one situation and refuse to speak or play with anyone in another situation.

Is Shyness a Problem?

Shyness itself is not a problem and many people do not consider shyness to be a problem. Some people are just naturally inclined to be by themselves or have just a few friends. Shyness is *not* a problem if a child is happy, has a few close friends, does well in school, attends some social activities such as birthday parties, and participates in some group activities such as soccer. Shyness is *not* a problem if other people do not mind a person's shyness or accept that person as he is. A child could be shy during a Scout activity but the group may still view the child in a positive way. Shyness is a natural part of many people, and that is okay.

Shyness *can* be a problem, however, if a child cannot do things she might normally like to do. *Excessive shyness is the target of this book* (Fig. 1.1). Some people are so shy they cannot interact well with others and so they stay by themselves. A child like Jaden might stay to the side of a playground at recess and not interact with anyone. Other children like Evan are so shy they are constantly anxious and upset around others. A child might not be able to enjoy a friend's birthday party because he feels nervous and nauseous. Shyness may also be a problem if it interferes with activities such as sleeping, eating, playing, and going to school.

Shyness might also be a problem if other people treat the child in a certain way. If a shy child is ridiculed, maltreated, neglected, or rejected by other children, this is a problem. If a shy child will not participate in any group or social activities and cannot make friends, this is a problem. If a shy child's avoidance of school or church or other important places causes much disruption and conflict for family members, this is a problem. Shyness can also be a problem if it is associated with mental disorders that perhaps need to be addressed by a qualified mental health professional (Box 1.1).

Box 1.1 Severe behavior related to shyness

Most overly shy kids have some distress in social situations but this distress can be managed using the methods in this book. Other shy children, however, show two very severe forms of behavior called social phobia and selective mutism. These conditions are at the far right end of the social discomfort spectrum in Figure 1.1.

Social phobia refers to very intense social anxiety or fear of social situations where embarrassment may occur. People with social phobia avoid many social situations or endure social situations with great dread. Social phobia occurs in about 18% of people who are shy. Children and adolescents with social phobia often refuse to go to school, are distressed and sad in many social situations, and have poor social skills and very few friends. Social phobia can lead to several long-term problems such as dependence on others, difficulty attending college or interacting with others, and depression. Children with social phobia should receive treatment from a qualified mental health professional.

Selective mutism refers to a child's failure to speak in public situations such as school, church, restaurants, parks, and stores. Children with selective mutism speak fine at home or around people with which they are comfortable. They do not usually have speech or language problems but sometimes have developmental delays. Some kids who are shy or who have social phobia also have selective mutism, but selective mutism itself affects about 1% of children. Selective mutism is a serious disorder that may need to be treated with the help of a qualified mental health professional and school officials. Methods to address children with aspects of selective mutism are discussed throughout this book and especially in Chapter 4.

Parents sometimes think of a shy child as stubborn or noncompliant, or think of their child's shyness as attention-seeking behavior. Some shy children can be stubborn and noncompliant, and can seek attention at times, but these behaviors are not the cause of a child's shyness. Shy children are quite uncomfortable in social situations and may thus seem resistant, clingy, willful, and whiny. As your overly shy child becomes more confident in social situations, many of these behaviors will improve. A child who is confident about approaching others, for example, will more easily go to a birthday party and will pester you less about feeling poorly.

Shy Children over Time

Shyness can be a serious issue because the behavior does increase the risk of certain problems over time. Shy children are at increased risk for anxiety disorders such as social phobia (Box 1.1) in adolescence. Shy children also tend to be lonelier than their peers over time. Adults who were shy as children tend to have unstable careers and marriages compared to most people. Men in particular tend to advance less in their careers if they are overly shy. Addressing your child's excessive shyness is thus an important goal of this book.

Consider some good news, however. Your child is not alone—many children are shy and some are overly shy, such as Tashi. Many overly shy children avoid social situations or have social skills that need improvement. Psychologists and other mental health professionals have been studying excessive shyness for decades and have a pretty good idea about how these children feel, think, and behave.

I have extensive experience working with shy and socially anxious children. I enjoy working with these children because of the great improvement they show. Excessive shyness can be managed! I have had success with many children. I have helped them lower anxiety, develop friendships, attend social gatherings, and perform well before others. This book includes specific and step-by-step methods to bring your child out of his shell and feel more confident and comfortable in social situations. You and your child can do it!

Will This Book Help Me?

This book will be more helpful for certain families than others (Table 1.1). Let's explore different topics to help you decide whether this book will be more or less helpful to you. First, this book will be more helpful if your child is actually shy! Some parents think their child is shy when actually he is not. If you are unsure, then review the definition of shyness and its parts mentioned earlier. If you feel your child is shy *and* his shyness seems to be a problem for him, then this book will be more useful to you.

Table 1.1 Will this book be helpful to you?

This book will be more helpful to you if:	This book will be less helpful to you if:
Your child is overly shy	Your child is not shy
Your child attends school regularly	Your child refuses school or has great trouble remaining in classes for an entire day
Your child does not have severe behavior problems	Your child has severe behavior problems such as attention deficit hyperactivity disorder, aggression, delinquent behavior, substance abuse, extreme anxiety and/or depression, and bipolar disorder
Your child avoids some social situations	Your child avoids all social situations and will not speak to anyone
Your child does not have a developmental disorder	Your child has a developmental disorder
Your child's shyness began at age 4 years or later	Your child has been intensely shy since birth
Your child is familiar with English	Your child is unfamiliar with English
Your child does not face school-based threats	Your child does face school-based threats
You, your partner, and your child agree to address overly shy behavior in a consistent way	You, your partner, and your child cannot agree to address overly shy behavior in a consistent way
You, your partner, or your child can put in significant effort to overcome excessive shyness	You, your partner, or your child cannot put in significant effort to overcome excessive shyness

This book will also be more useful to you if your child attends school regularly and does not have attendance problems or distress about being in school. This book will be less helpful, however, if your child misses many days of school or is extremely distressed about being in school (Box 1.2). In the latter case, you may wish to visit a qualified mental health professional.

Box 1.2 What if my child refuses to go to school?

Some kids have such strong social or performance anxiety or overwhelming shyness that they have trouble attending school. If your child is missing many days of school, then visit a qualified mental health professional. If your child misses school only occasionally, then the methods in this book and elsewhere may be helpful. One resource for parents of youths who refuse school is a self-directed book called "*Getting Your Child to Say 'Yes' to School: A Guide for Parents of Youths with School Refusal Behavior,*" by the author of this book (Kearney) and published by Oxford University Press. This book offers suggestions for parents of youth who refuse school for different reasons, including reasons related to social and performance anxiety.

Insist that your child attend school daily. Do not allow shyness to be a reason for missing school, especially if your child usually goes to school. Even if your child is not actively participating in school, he can still attend each class, do his homework, and get good grades. As he does so, he and you will work together with school officials to manage excessive shyness and increase positive social and performance behaviors.

If your child complains of headaches, stomachaches, or other bodily problems from having to attend school, then pursue a full medical examination to rule out or treat any physical disorders. Some children do have minor physical symptoms because of social- or performance-related stress, but these symptoms are not usually strong enough to justify staying home from school. A child should go to school unless he has vomiting, high fever, severe diarrhea, bleeding, lice, or intense pain or flu-like symptoms. If a child has minor physical problems during the day, he may visit the school nurse but should stay in school.

This book will also be more useful to you if your child and your family generally have fewer and less severe problems and if your child's shyness is his *main and sole concern*. If your child is shy *and* has other problems such as general noncompliance (not listening) at home, then the book will be less helpful. If your child is shy and has severe behavior problems such as attention deficit hyperactivity disorder or extreme depression, then this book may be less helpful. If this is the case, then you may wish to visit a qualified mental health professional.

This book will be more helpful to you if your child's shyness is *not* severe. If your child can talk to people to some extent, even if quietly, then this book will be more helpful. If your child avoids many situations and will not speak to anyone, then this book will be less helpful. In a related fashion, some children who are excessively shy have developmental disorders related to autism, Asperger's disorder, or mental retardation. These disorders refer to delays in social, intellectual, academic, or language development (Chapter 7). Children with these disorders will benefit less from this book, so I recommend a broader plan developed with educational and mental health professionals.

This book will be more helpful to you if your child's shyness first developed around age 4–5 years or later. Some parents report intense shyness in their child seemingly since birth, which may indicate a more severe and inhibited form of shyness. Shyness tends to be less severe if it developed a bit later in life, such as when a child started kindergarten. The methods described in this book will be more helpful for these less severe instances of shyness.

This book will be more helpful to you if your child's language matches that of his peers at school and in many social situations. Some families speak to their child only in Spanish, Tagalog, or Mandarin at home but the child is surrounded by English-speaking peers and teachers at school. This may cause some children to withdraw or become less confident in social situations. This book will be less helpful if a child is relatively unfamiliar with English and does not practice English at home.

This book will be more helpful to you if family members generally get along with one other. This book will be less helpful if you and your partner argue a lot about many things. If you are currently involved in a child custody dispute, then this book will be less helpful as well. To help an overly shy child, *parents must develop a united front that includes mutual support*. Furthermore, if you or your partner have significant anxiety, depression, substance use, or other problems, then this book will be less helpful. If this is the case, then you may wish to visit a qualified mental health professional.

This book will be more helpful to you if your shy child does *not* face legitimate threats from others. Some children want to avoid many social situations at school, for example, because of true school-based threats. True school-based threats include *excessive teasing, taunting, bullying, verbal or physical assaults or intimidation, theft, property damage, and sexual or other maltreatment from peers, school officials, or others*. This book will not be helpful for children who avoid such threats (you and I would not go to such a place either!). If a child avoids school or social situations because he does not want to face these threats, then the threats must be resolved *before* trying the methods in this book.

Parents, school officials, and others should work to resolve true school-based threats. Solutions may include removing a bully or threat from school and *reducing the social isolation of the victim*. Every instance of bullying must be reported and dealt with swiftly. Children should travel to school with friends and encourage school officials to better monitor potential threats and actively work to prevent them. If a bullying or an otherwise threatening situation is adequately resolved and a child *still* avoids school-based social situations, then this book will be more helpful. Some children continue to avoid school-based social situations even after a bully has been sent to another school.

The Structure of This Book

This chapter is devoted to helping you understand what shyness is as well as some common problems that come with this behavior. Chapter 2 is designed to help you better understand why your child is shy and how you can keep track of your child's behavior. Chapter 2 also contains an overview of various methods described in this book to help your overly shy child interact with others and feel less distress.

Specific methods for helping your overly shy child are covered in Chapters 3–6. Chapter 3 focuses on what you as a parent can do on a daily basis at home to help your overly shy child. Chapter 4 focuses on how an overly shy child can learn to approach different social and performance situations in community and school settings and how you can work with school officials to improve your child's interactions with others. Chapter 5 focuses on social skills that some overly shy children need to practice, such as better eye contact and voice volume. Chapter 6 focuses on how an overly shy child can manage anxiety in different social situations. Examples include learning to relax and changing worrisome thoughts. Chapter 7 focuses on ways to prevent problems in the future so your overly shy child can continue to interact with or perform before others with less distress.

I strongly encourage you (and your child) to *read each chapter in this book*. You may feel your overly shy child has good social skills, for example, but I recommend reading Chapter 5 anyway. You will likely find some valuable information in each chapter that you and your child can use every day.

Defining Success

How do you know if this book worked for you? Success is sometimes hard to define for overly shy children, but one obvious thing to look at is whether a child can talk to others and attend group functions. As your shy child becomes more skilled in different social situations, he should be able to introduce himself to others, participate in class and in meetings, perform before others, and stay longer at fun activities such as birthday parties. You should notice that your child avoids situations less than before and finds social activities to be more rewarding and fun.

Your child should also become less distressed or worried in social situations. She should be more confident about handling different social situations and managing anxiety. She should be more independent of help from others, so you should see less crying, reassurance-seeking, and clinging. She should be able to think more realistically in social situations and realize that terrible consequences are usually not going to happen.

Success will not be defined by a total change in personality. As mentioned earlier, shyness is a stable trait. Most children who are shy or introverted remain that way, and that is okay. Again, simple shyness is not a problem. Shyness associated with avoidance of social situations and great distress *is* a problem, however. This book is designed to help your overly shy child become more skillful in social situations and less distressed so he can have friends and experience a good quality of life.

What If I Try the Methods in This Book and Nothing Happens?

If you try the methods in this book and they do not seem to help, then one of several things might be happening (see also Chapter 7). First, your situation may not completely fit the purpose of this book, so different or more extensive procedures may be necessary. The methods discussed in this book can be done under the guidance of a qualified mental health professional who can help you address more intense issues such as attention deficit hyperactivity disorder or persistent school refusal behavior (Box 1.3).

Box 1.3 Considering a qualified mental health professional

If you believe this book would be less helpful for you for the reasons listed in Table 1.1, then consider seeing a qualified mental health professional. A *clinical child psychologist* has specialized training with youths with severe behavior problems. A *psychiatrist* is a medical doctor who can prescribe medication for severe behavior problems. For many children with severe behavior problems that significantly interfere with daily life, seeing both a clinical child psychologist and a psychiatrist is a good idea.

If you decide to seek a mental health professional in your area, then consult with local people who are knowledgeable about who specializes in certain kinds of problems. Some mental health professionals have special training in substance abuse or depression. Others work closely with school officials to help resolve problems such as learning disorders, attention deficit hyperactivity disorder, or intense school refusal behavior. Consulting with the psychology faculty at a local university is a good start when trying to find someone who best fits your situation. If you live in an area where this is not possible, contact your state associations of psychologists and psychiatrists. Talk to guidance counselors and other professionals at your child's school who work with certain therapists. You may also consult the websites of national associations of mental health professionals, such as apa.org, abct.org, and psych.org.

Second, you or your child may have tried the methods in this book for only a short time. The methods in this book must be carried out for an extensive period, perhaps several weeks or months. Shyness is an ingrained behavior and excessive shyness takes time to overcome. Parents and children need to understand as well that the skills and methods covered in this book must continue to be practiced during their lifetime.

Third, everyone must be on the same page. The skills and methods in this book will work only if you, your partner, your child, and school officials (if necessary) work together on a set plan. If one parent helps a shy child meet other people but the other parent allows the child to miss a birthday party, for example, then the methods described here will be less helpful. *Consistent effort and practice from everyone is a major key to success.*

Communicating with School Officials

If you feel this book might be helpful to you and that it applies to your situation, then let's get started! I have some things to ask you to do to set the groundwork for what is to come. Helping your overly shy child will likely mean talking to school officials such as your child's guidance counselor, teachers, school psychologist, school-based social worker, or principal or dean. *Frequent communication between parents and school officials is necessary and essential.*

I recommend obtaining the contact information for as many school-related people as possible. In Worksheet 1.1, write down important contact information for yourself, your partner, your child, and relevant school officials. This information should include cell phone numbers and email addresses because school officials are busy and sometimes hard to contact. Have this information handy at all times. This is especially important if your child misses school because of excessive shyness.

I also suggest that you schedule a face-to-face meeting with your child's teacher(s) and guidance counselor. You may have already done this, but before using any of the methods in this book you should do so again and let school officials know what you plan on doing. *To help an overly shy child interact with others with less distress, parents and school officials must be on the same page.* If you have not already done

Worksheet 1.1 Contact information

Me

My partner

My child (cell phone number most likely)

Close family relatives who live nearby and others (e.g., neighbors, friends) who can help

My child's guidance counselor

My child's teacher(s)

My child's principal/dean

My child's school psychologist or school-based social worker

My child's school nurse

My child's school attendance officer

so, please speak with school officials about the following types of information:

- Extracurricular activities in which your child could participate
- Feedback from school officials about their willingness to help you address your overly shy child when he is at school, such as managing anxiety and practicing skills in social situations
- Situations your child avoids at school such as eating in the cafeteria
- Teasing, bullying, or other school-based threats if relevant
- Time missed from class or days missed from school if relevant
- Your child's conversations with peers, classmates, and adults at school
- Your child's performance before others such as writing or reading before others, dressing and performing in physical education class, or singing or otherwise performing musically.
- Your child's social behavior in class, on the playground, during group activities, in the cafeteria, walking in hallways, and before and after school
- Your suggested plan for helping your overly shy child based on methods described in this book (once you have read the book!)

Develop a good relationship with your child's teacher, guidance counselor, and/or other relevant school officials. Be prepared to work with your child at school if officials there are overburdened. Shy and anxious children are sometimes overlooked because much attention must be given to disruptive or aggressive children. Excessive shyness can be as painful and devastating as acting-out behavior problems, and this is a point that sometimes needs to be impressed on school officials.

What Is Next?

Now that you have everyone's contact information and have spoken with school officials, begin reading Chapter 2. In Chapter 2, I discuss in more detail what causes excessive shyness and how overly shy children progress from childhood to adolescence. I also cover ways you can monitor your child's shy behaviors and get a better understanding of the parts of her shyness. Chapter 2 also contains a more detailed overview of the methods in this book to help your overly shy child improve his performance in social situations.

2

Monitoring Your Child's Social Behavior

Jessica is a 7-year-old girl in first grade who works well in school but prefers to play with just one or two friends at recess. She gets along well with her two friends, Jenna and Jackie, but tends to play by herself and is hesitant to speak to others when her friends are not around or when they do not wish to play with her. Jessica is sometimes withdrawn, especially at lunch when she eats quietly and speaks infrequently and softly.

McKenna is a 12-year-old girl in sixth grade who is beginning to struggle a bit academically at school because her assignments require more group cooperation and presentation before others. Her classmates seem to like McKenna, but they say she declines offers to play and does not offer much verbal input in academic tasks. McKenna has cried twice at school and prefers to be by herself.

Grant is a 17-year-old boy in high school who becomes upset and experiences strong social anxiety when having to interact with peers and teachers at school. He avoids many social and performance situations, remains quiet, seems sad, has no friends, and participates little in class. Grant seems motivated to remain as "invisible" as possible by sitting in the back of his classes, slouching, eating his lunch outside by himself, and even skipping some classes.

This chapter will cover the following topics:

- Explore why some children are overly shy and how shyness can change over time.

- Discuss ways to monitor your child's excessive shyness.
- Provide an overview of the methods in this book to overcome excessive shyness.

Recall from Chapter 1 that shyness refers to possible physical discomfort around others, concerns or worry about evaluations from others, and a tendency to withdraw from social situations and to pursue solitary activities. Remember that *shyness itself is not a bad thing*. Many children are shy but still have some friends, do well in school, are liked by others, and do not seem distressed. *Excessive shyness*, however, can lead to loneliness, academic problems, sadness, alienation from peers, and substantial distress. This book addresses *excessive shyness*, such as the type shown by Jessica, McKenna, and Grant.

Parents ask me all the time: What causes my child to be so shy or socially anxious? Is it my fault? Did I do something wrong? Shyness is actually caused by many different reasons, as summarized below. Some of these reasons are specific to a child, some involve parent and family interactions, and some involve peer interactions or even cultural expectations. Excessive shyness is not anyone's fault, but examining the different reasons why a child is excessively shy is important for understanding how and why different methods are helpful in overcoming this problem.

What Causes Shyness?

Excessive shyness can be caused by many different factors, but the main ones are summarized here. Shyness is a *temperament*, or early personality characteristic, that does seem to run in families. Some genetic component may thus be involved. Many children who are overly shy often have one or both parents (or other relatives) who are shy, meek, or softspoken themselves, which is fine. Working with a child with excessive shyness often means that parents have to be closely involved in the process.

This section summarizes key factors other than genetics that relate to excessive shyness. These include child-, parent-, and peer-related factors as well as culture. I point out how these factors relate to different methods described later in this book. Let's first discuss some child-related reasons for excessive shyness. These include behavioral inhibition, worrisome thoughts, and learning experiences.

Behavioral Inhibition

One child characteristic that seems related to excessive shyness and social anxiety is *behavioral inhibition*. Behavioral inhibition refers to fearfulness, timidity, avoidance, and guardedness in response to new objects or social situations. This means that some children—about 10–15%—react anxiously when faced with new situations, peers, or social interactions. Behavioral inhibition can be seen in infants who cry excessively, act fearful, and move around a lot when they encounter someone they have never seen before. Keep in mind that such a reaction is normal in children younger than age 2 years, but is more unusual in preschoolers. A child with behavioral inhibition may become very upset when faced with something or someone who is unfamiliar and he may seem fearful, say very little, withdraw, and frown. Behavioral inhibition is seen in many children who are overly shy, but is *not* characteristic of *all* children who are overly shy.

Children with excessive shyness or social anxiety may have other temperamental characteristics as well. Some children with excessive shyness are often sad, anxious, and overaroused. Grant, for example, became quite upset when faced with the prospect of interacting with others at school. Other children with excessive shyness feel they *lack control* over key elements of their lives. These children may see social and performance situations as unpredictable or uncontrollable and feel their own social behavior has little effect on others. McKenna may believe, for example, that any attempt to strike up a conversation with a classmate will result in rejection. Other children with excessive shyness have trouble controlling their own emotions during social and performance situations. Children such as Grant may experience strong anger or anxiety or fear during interactions with others, which can be quite unpleasant. They then avoid social and performance situations so they do not have to experience these strong emotions.

Characteristics such as anxiety, overarousal, and difficulty controlling strong emotions can sometimes lead to unpleasant physical symptoms such as muscle tension, hyperventilation, and other symptoms mentioned in Chapter 1. Methods to help children relax and breathe properly in social and performance situations are presented in Chapter 6. Temperamental characteristics can also overlap with worrisome thoughts, which are discussed next.

Worrisome Thoughts

Recall from Chapter 1 that some children with excessive shyness or social anxiety also have worrisome thoughts about social and performance situations that are not accurate. Many of these children believe that terrible things will happen in social situations (especially embarrassment or humiliation) or think wrongly about how others are judging them. Older children and adolescents with excessive shyness may do the following as well:

- Assume that external events are their fault when this is not the case.
- Assume that one bad event means all such events will be negative.
- Believe that events are either good or bad, with no middle ground.
- Believe that social interactions are dangerous or threatening.
- Believe the world "should" operate a certain way.
- Believe they will always be excluded or ignored by others.
- Believe they will appear foolish, nervous, incompetent, or inadequate before others.
- Dismiss positive events, such as a compliment, as negative or trivial.
- Evaluate a situation as much worse than it really is.
- Focus much more on the negative than the positive in a social situation.
- Make a conclusion about a social situation that is not realistic or based on evidence.
- Predict future terrible events such as ridicule even without supporting evidence.
- Remember negative aspects of a situation and forget positive ones.

McKenna believed others would respond negatively to her if she spoke to them. She thought classmates would laugh or ridicule her voice. Thoughts such as these can prolong a child's shyness because she declines to speak and does not see that her thought is inaccurate. McKenna often avoids verbal interactions with classmates and thus does not see that her peers are not likely to laugh at her voice. I discuss ways to help children such as McKenna manage worrisome thoughts in Chapter 6. Worrisome thoughts can sometimes interact with negative learning experiences, which are discussed next.

Learning Experiences

A child's learning experiences can also influence his excessive shyness. Some children report negative social experiences that involved bullying, victimization, teasing, ridicule, embarrassment, or humiliation. A child could be assaulted at school, ridiculed during an oral presentation, or publicly degraded. Negative experiences can reinforce a child's shyness. If McKenna were to speak to some classmates who then ridiculed her, then this would reinforce her social withdrawal. Other children who were not previously shy could also become more socially withdrawn or even refuse to go to school because of a traumatic social event. Some children with excessive shyness do not experience events such as these because their shyness forces them to withdraw from many social interactions. However, those who socially isolate themselves are at risk of being bullied or otherwise victimized.

Parent and Family-Based Reasons

Parents and families can also contribute to a child's excessive shyness. One contributing factor involves parents who allow their shy child to avoid or escape from many social and performance situations. Parents who acquiesce to a child's demands to stay home rather than go to a birthday party or soccer practice reward their child's avoidance. Other parents "rescue" a child who wishes to escape social interactions by removing him from a social activity. Children also learn at an early age that illness helps them avoid social obligations, and some parents are sensitive to headaches and stomachaches that suddenly appear when a child has to go to school or speak to others. Other parents discourage their children from participating in social and extracurricular activities or are very restrictive about allowing a child to associate with others.

Parents can also do other things to aggravate a child's shyness. Some parents are very sensitive to the opinions and negative evaluations of others, and children pick up on that. Other parents avoid social situations themselves, which models social avoidance for their child, or are overprotective of their child. A good rule of thumb is that a family that socializes a lot with others will tend to have children who socialize a lot with others. Even shy children usually develop and practice good social skills during these many social contacts. Parents can also contribute to a child's social withdrawal by fighting a lot, ridiculing a child, or expressing shame about their child's shyness. A better approach is to gently encourage a child to engage with others, a practice covered in more depth in Chapters 3 and 4.

Other Reasons

Excessive shyness or social avoidance can also be due to other reasons. Children who become socially withdrawn, for example, may be experiencing depression, trauma, or pain or another medical condition. A child who was not normally socially withdrawn but suddenly becomes so should be evaluated by a qualified mental health professional (Chapter 1). Serious issues such as suicidality, maltreatment, or substance use should be considered in sudden cases of social withdrawal. Some children who are overly shy also lack social skills, or ways to communicate effectively with others. Important social skills include eye contact, audible voice, and maintaining a conversation. Social skills improvement is a key feature of Chapter 5.

A child's classmates or other peers can also influence his excessive shyness. I mentioned victimization and teasing, but peers who neglect or reject a child can also contribute to social withdrawal. Of course, this is often a cycle that repeats itself—a shy child may avoid contacts with others who then neglect the child or feel the child is rejecting them. The child may then believe that others do not want to play and then withdraw even further, which reinforces the cycle. Helping excessively shy children come out of their shell will involve arranging specific social and performance situations with peers and others where interactions are practiced extensively. This process will be covered in Chapters 3 and 4.

Culture is another important part of shyness. Shyness is sometimes considered a problem or an oddity in Western societies that emphasize individualism and assertiveness. These cultures may consider shyness as a negative characteristic. Other cultures, however, especially Asian cultures, view shyness and social reticence as positive traits. Shy children in Asian cultures are often viewed as intelligent and successful and many Asian parents encourage socially inhibited behavior. A child's cultural background and family values should thus be considered when thinking about shyness.

Shyness thus relates to different genetic, child, parent, peer, and cultural factors. Knowing why your child is overly shy is not vital, however.

The methods in this book apply to all children who are overly shy regardless of most causes. I also recommend that you accept your child's temperament—children who are shy generally remain shy, and that is okay. The goal is *not* to transform your shy child into a social butterfly and extrovert. But some overly shy children have a sad or lonely life. The methods in this book will help improve your overly shy child's quality of life.

How Does Shyness Change over Time?

Shyness can be a stable trait that begins early in life and continues throughout life. A shy child is likely to be a shy adolescent and a shy adult. Again, simple shyness is not a problem and we do not want to reduce your child's shyness level to zero! Shyness can, however, change or worsen over time to become excessive and to include social anxiety, and this should be addressed. Let's discuss a sample sequence to illustrate this process (Fig. 2.1).

Imagine a preschooler who has some behavioral inhibition, meaning he becomes upset when faced with unfamiliar situations or people. The child may be fussy, clingy, and demanding in these situations, such as entering a new day care, being with a babysitter, or attending a birthday party. The child may isolate himself in these situations, preferring to play alone at day care, or throw tantrums or otherwise act defiantly to leave a situation and go home. This behavior could be rewarded by parents who agree to take the child home, do not place the child in social situations in which he may act up, or respond to the child's misbehaviors inappropriately (e.g., excessive discipline or lack of discipline).

These early child–parent interactions can lead to fewer social interactions and less chance for the child to develop important social skills and receive feedback from others. A child pulled from preschool or interactions with peers, for example, has less chance to learn how to engage appropriately with others and to receive feedback from others about proper play behaviors or aggression. The child may then become more anxious when in a social situation and increase his misbehavior to avoid these situations.

As this child enters elementary school, he is faced with many demands that include social interaction and academic and athletic performance. A child who does not have much skill interacting with

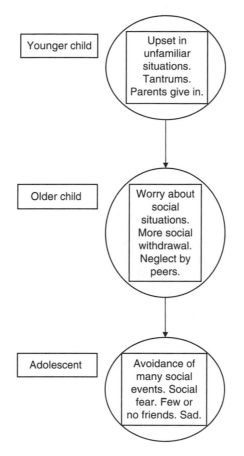

Figure 2.1. Sample developmental progression of excessive shyness.

peers may withdraw during these situations and experience neglect or rejection from his peers. The child's social anxiety may increase and he may avoid social situations more frequently. This process could worsen with time if social situations outside of school become less frequent, if parents and teachers do not intervene to correct the behavior, or if peers ridicule or otherwise torment the child.

Consider Jessica, McKenna, and Grant. You can see that their social interaction problems worsened with age. The younger Jessica played with a few friends, for example, but McKenna generally avoided social interactions and Grant was outright fearful of others and had no friends. In addition, Jessica and McKenna attended school but Grant was skipping some classes. Jessica and McKenna seem to be liked by their peers, but Grant was determined to be as "invisible" as possible at school. Sadness increased with age as well, perhaps as a result of their social isolation.

Monitoring Your Child's Excessive Shyness

You will find throughout this book that I ask you to watch your child carefully to see if he is progressing. I outline different methods of doing so in this section. First, though, I recommend considering the answers to some basic questions to help you understand what you should watch for most:

- Does my child want to avoid most social situations?
- Does my child cry, throw a tantrum, or show other behavior problems when faced with the prospect of interacting with others?
- Does my child seem very anxious or sad when interacting with others?
- Does my child withdraw, cringe, or shrink from others, especially those he does not know well?
- Does my child mostly want to be around only family members or people he knows well?
- Does my child have great difficulty performing before others in some way, such as athletically, academically, musically, or otherwise?
- Does my child have many worrisome thoughts about interacting with others?
- Does my child have many physical complaints when around others, such as headaches, stomachaches, pain, "butterflies" in the stomach, or shakiness?
- Does my child have trouble knowing how to interact with others, such as maintaining an extended conversation?
- Does my child have very few or no friends?
- Does my child refuse to speak, or is he unwilling to speak, in public situations?
- Does my child refuse to go to school or skip classes because of concerns about social and performance situations there?
- Do my child's shy behaviors prevent him from doing things he would like to do or should be doing?

If the answer to some or many of these questions is "yes," then your child may be excessively shy. Even if the answer to a few of these questions is yes, then the methods in this book will be helpful. Some excessively shy children, for example, do not have any physical complaints or tantrums but seem sad and have few if any friends. Other children seem quite distressed when meeting people for the first time but are fine when interacting with people they know well. If shy behaviors seem to interfere with what your child would like to do or should be doing, such as going to school, then the behaviors may be a problem. Be sure that any questions to which you answered "yes" are part of your regular monitoring process, which is discussed next.

Monitoring different aspects of your child's shyness is important for several reasons because doing so will help you with the following:

- Become more aware of your child's interactions with, and performance before, others.
- Become more aware of your child's level of distress in social and performance situations.
- See how your child's behavior changes during the week.
- Chart whether your child's level of social avoidance improves with time.
- Find out why your child has difficulty speaking to or performing before others.
- See whether the methods in this book are indeed working.
- Share important information about your child's excessive shyness with others such as teachers and other school officials.
- Look for signs that your child's excessive shyness may be recurring after he begins to speak well to others and perform well before others.

The important behaviors that you should monitor each week include your child's interactions with or performances before others, his level of distress in these situations, and his level of social avoidance. Let's discuss these separately.

Interactions with Others

If you are reading this book, then increasing the number of interactions your child has with others may be one of your most important goals. We must therefore know the number of social and performance situations in which your child seems excessively shy. Consider Worksheet 2.1. This worksheet lists common social and performance situations

Worksheet 2.1 Does your child seem excessively shy in the following situations?

Home	Overly shy? Y/N	Level of distress (0-10)	Level of avoidance (0-10)
Answering the door or telephone	_____	_____	_____
Speaking to parents	_____	_____	_____
Speaking to siblings	_____	_____	_____
Speaking to visitors your child knows well	_____	_____	_____
Speaking to visitors your child does not know well	_____	_____	_____
Speaking to peers inside the home with parents present	_____	_____	_____
Talking on the telephone with a friend or familiar relative	_____	_____	_____
Talking on the telephone with an unfamiliar person	_____	_____	_____

Community/public	Overly shy? Y/N	Level of distress (0-10)	Level of avoidance (0-10)
Asking someone out on a date	_____	_____	_____
Being assertive with someone	_____	_____	_____
Being introduced to new people	_____	_____	_____
Expressing an opinion to other people	_____	_____	_____
Going to a party or similar social gathering	_____	_____	_____
Going to an extracurricular activity	_____	_____	_____
Inviting a friend to an activity	_____	_____	_____
Ordering food	_____	_____	_____
Speaking to parents or siblings in markets and similar places	_____	_____	_____

	Overly shy? Y/N	Level of distress (0-10)	Level of avoidance (0-10)
Speaking to peers at social events or extracurricular activities	____	____	____
Speaking to other adults in public situations	____	____	____
Speaking to clerks or waiters	____	____	____

School	Overly shy? Y/N	Level of distress (0-10)	Level of avoidance (0-10)
Answering a question in class	____	____	____
Asking the teacher a question in class	____	____	____
Attending physical education class	____	____	____
Eating in the school cafeteria	____	____	____
Participating in a group or team project at school	____	____	____
Playing a musical instrument or singing before others	____	____	____
Playing with peers on the playground	____	____	____
Reading before classmates	____	____	____
Speaking to peers on the playground	____	____	____
Speaking to peers in hallways and related situations	____	____	____
Speaking to peers in the classroom	____	____	____
Speaking to peers at lunch/cafeteria	____	____	____
Speaking to peers on the school bus	____	____	____
Speaking to parents at school	____	____	____
Speaking to teachers on the playground	____	____	____
Speaking to teachers in the classroom	____	____	____
Speaking to other staff members at school	____	____	____
Speaking during academic activities	____	____	____
Speaking before classmates	____	____	____
Taking a test	____	____	____

Continued

Worksheet 2.1 cont'd

	Overly shy? Y/N	Level of distress (0-10)	Level of avoidance (0-10)
School			
Using the restroom at school	_____	_____	_____
Walking in the hallway at school	_____	_____	_____
Writing on the blackboard in class	_____	_____	_____
	Overly shy? Y/N	Level of distress (0-10)	Level of avoidance (0-10)
Other social or performance situations			
_____	_____	_____	_____
_____	_____	_____	_____
_____	_____	_____	_____
_____	_____	_____	_____
_____	_____	_____	_____

NOTE: Level of distress/avoidance: 0=none, 5=moderate, 10=extreme.

your child may encounter during the day. These situations could occur at home, school, or in community settings such as restaurants, shopping malls, grocery stores, or parks. Some of these situations may not apply to your child, so ignore irrelevant ones. For the others, go down the list carefully and write a "Y" in the "Y/N?" column if your child seems overly shy in that situation. If your child is overly shy in just a few situations, that is fine.

Your child may also be overly shy in some situations that are not on this list. If so, write this situation in the blank spaces at the bottom of the worksheet. Do not include situations that your child rarely encounters, such as not wanting to go trick-or-treating on Halloween. Instead, stick to situations that occur at least a few times each week and that cause some distress for your child. Worksheet 2.1 lists situations in which many overly shy children have problems, but your child may have some specific daily interaction that gives him trouble. We certainly want to include that type of situation.

I recommend reviewing this list *at least once per week*. You may find that your child's shyness changes somewhat from week to week or that a new situation gives your child some trouble. Some children, for example, report fluctuating problems at physical education class depending on what activity is required. An overly shy child may have less difficulty with an individual sport such as swimming than with a team sport such as football. Reviewing the list at least once per week also allows you to monitor your child's progress and see whether the number of difficult situations decreases over time.

Level of Distress in Social and Performance Situations

Another important point to monitor is the level of distress your child feels in social and performance situations. *Distress refers to how anxious, stressed, upset, nervous, fearful, or sad your child feels in these situations.* Different children with excessive shyness have different reactions to social and performance situations—some are anxious, some simply withdraw or cringe, and some become sad and cry. Some children have many physical symptoms such as shakiness and some have many worrisome thoughts about how others will judge them. What does your excessively shy child do that indicates she is distressed, especially in these situations? Complete the sections that follow to obtain a better understanding of your child's distress in social and performance situations:

What my child "feels" when distressed (physical symptoms)

_____

_____

_____

_____

What my child "thinks" (or says) when distressed (worrisome thoughts)

_____

_____

_____

_____

Note the middle column in Worksheet 2.1. This column includes a rating of distress that ranges from 0 to 10. Zero (0) indicates no distress at all, 5 indicates a moderate amount of distress, and 10 indicates an extreme amount of distress. Of course, any number from 0 to 10 can be given. If you provided a "Y" next to a key social or performance situation on the list, then provide a rating of your child's overall distress (i.e., physical symptoms and worrisome thoughts) in that situation.

I recommend doing this with your child because children are sometimes better at knowing their level of distress in a given situation. I also recommend speaking to others who interact with your child, especially teachers and school officials, relatives, siblings, and peers and friends. Try to obtain as accurate a rating as possible.

Review these ratings *at least once per week* but daily if possible. You want to look for spikes or troughs in your child's ratings. You may find, for example, that your child's distress is high at school but not at home or in community settings. Or, you may find that your child's distress is high in the morning at school but not in the afternoon. The more specific you can be about your child's distress the more you can use the methods in this book in efficient ways. If your child is primarily distressed during two classes at school, for example, then you could work with your child and with school officials to practice the methods in this book mostly during those classes.

Avoidance of Social and Performance Situations

The last important piece of information we want to know about your child's excessive shyness is how much she actively avoids social or performance situations. The last column of Worksheet 2.1 allows you to rate how much your child *avoids* a particular situation. The avoidance rating is the same as the distress rating: zero (0) indicates no avoidance, 5 indicates a moderate amount of avoidance, and 10 indicates an extreme amount of avoidance. Of course, any number from 0 to 10 can be given. If you provided a "Y" next to a key social or performance situation on the list, then provide a rating of your child's avoidance in that situation.

Your rating of your child's avoidance in a given situation does not have to be the same as your rating of your child's distress in that situation. Some children, for example, have great distress speaking to peers at school but do not avoid this situation. Other children avoid a certain situation and thus do not have much distress about it. As with the first two columns, I recommend reviewing your avoidance ratings with your child *at least once per week.* As with shyness situations and distress, avoidance can fluctuate and we want to see whether the methods in this book are having an effect.

You may also wish to think about what *sequences of behaviors* lead to your child's avoidance of social situations. Consider Figure 2.2.

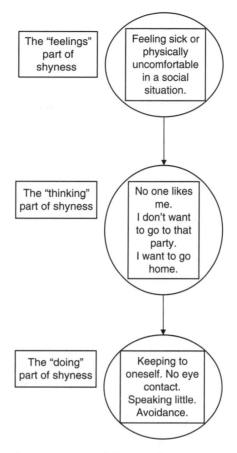

Figure 2.2. Sample sequence of shyness behaviors.

In this case, a child's anxious feelings lead to worries that lead to avoidance. A child may feel sick about going to karate class, for example, tell his mother that he does not want to perform his kicks in class before others, and ask to stay home. Other shy children have certain worries that then lead to physical symptoms and then avoidance. What does your overly shy child do?

Information from Teachers

You may find it useful to collect information from your child's teacher(s) regarding how your child interacts with others or performs before

Worksheet 2.2 Daily report card

Date: _____

Social or performance situations avoided today

Level of distress shown by child today (use 0-10 scale)

X----- X------ X ------X------ X------ X ------X------ X------X ------X------X

0	1	2	3	4	5	6	7	8	9	10
None		A little		Some		Stronger		A lot		The worst

Behavior problems in school today

Other comments

_____

others at school. I recommend using some form of *daily report card* to get this information (see Worksheet 2.2). Teachers are busy people, so I recommend keeping the daily report card as simple as possible. The one illustrated here allows your child's teacher to quickly provide information about social or performance situations your child avoided that day as well as a rating of his distress at school. The teacher can also provide information about special behavior problems or other issues that arose that day that would be of interest to you. Feel free to modify this worksheet as necessary to fit your child's behaviors at school.

Methods to Address Excessive Shyness

You will find various methods in this book that you and your child can practice to address excessive shyness and related problems. These methods will focus greatly on reducing your child's distress and avoidance in social and performance situations and improving his effectiveness in those situations. Different methods are needed to address the different parts of excessive shyness.

An important part of this process will be to have your child practice different social and performance behaviors in various settings. This practice will largely involve the items you endorsed in Worksheet 2.1. Chapters 3 and 4 concentrate heavily on this practice and represent the heart of this book. These chapters include specific suggestions to help your child speak to others effectively. But this approach must be a gradual one—we cannot ask your child to speak to many people all at once. Chapter 3 thus focuses on things you can do on a regular, everyday basis near home to improve your child's effectiveness in social situations. Some of these things are as simple as giving feedback to your child as he speaks to you. Some shy children speak very softly, so parents can encourage a child to speak more clearly and audibly so everyone can hear him.

Chapter 4 includes step-by-step instructions for arranging certain social and performance situations that your child can practice independently in community and school settings. These situations will mirror those you and your child endorsed in Worksheet 2.1. For example, you may work with your child's teacher to arrange situations in which your child will be expected to introduce himself to a new classmate, write on the blackboard, or participate more in physical education class. The more your child practices these situations the more effective and less shy he will be over time. I also discuss ways to address children with selective mutism more in Chapter 4.

I mentioned that many children with excessive shyness also have trouble with social skills such as establishing good eye contact, speaking clearly and audibly, and maintaining a conversation with others. Many overly shy children avoid social situations and do not have much practice developing these skills. As a result, they may avoid more social situations because they do not feel confident in their ability to interact with others. Chapter 5 focuses on ways to help your child develop important social skills and increase his confidence in different situations.

Another part of excessive shyness is physical symptoms of nervousness that children have around others. These symptoms may include muscle tension, shakiness or jitteriness, shortness of breath, hyperventilation, or general achiness (Chapter 1). Chapter 6 includes methods to help children overcome or manage these symptoms. This chapter focuses on relaxation training, or tensing and releasing different muscle groups in the arms, torso, legs, face, and other areas to help a child feel more at ease when interacting with others. Chapter 6 also focuses on breathing retraining, or establishing more regular breathing to ease tension and control hyperventilation. Relaxation training and breathing retraining can be used when a child practices social behaviors (Chapters 3 and 4).

Chapter 6 also includes suggestions to help your child change worrisome thoughts she has during social interactions. As mentioned earlier, some overly shy children believe a situation is much worse than it really is, assume wrongly what others are thinking, or worry too much about possible negative consequences of speaking to others. This may lead to avoidance. Chapter 6 includes methods to help your child change worrisome thoughts and enter social and performance situations with more confidence.

After your child has progressed and is speaking well with others, we want to make sure we maintain these gains. Chapter 7 thus focuses on ways to help your child keep up the good work and continue to be effective in social and performance situations. Chapter 7 also includes recommendations for pursuing formal treatment if needed and a discussion of special circumstances that sometimes accompany children with excessive shyness. These special circumstances include developmental or communication disorders, depression, trauma, multiple children with shyness, perfectionism, medication, and teasing and bullying.

What Is Next?

Now that you and your child have learned about excessive shyness and its various parts, it is time to do something about it! I mentioned that we want to start slowly and help your child gradually become more social, so we begin with small, everyday things you and your child can do together near home to boost his ability to interact with others and his confidence in interacting with others. This process begins in Chapter 3.

3

Home-Based Practice

Hunter is a 9-year-old boy in fourth grade who is excessively shy. He will occasionally speak to certain friends and teachers but only in a soft voice that they sometimes cannot hear. Hunter prefers to work alone and runs near other children on the playground but does not actively participate in games. He is also quiet at home but has recently been more vocal with his mother, asking her repeatedly to keep him home from school.

This chapter will cover the following topics:

- Reward your child for doing things necessary to overcome his shyness.
- Encourage your child to interact with others and perform before others.
- Examine how you speak to your child.
- Work with school officials to reward social behavior.
- Avoid common pitfalls such as rewarding inappropriate behavior.

We have discussed what shyness is and how shyness can become severe or chronic during a child's life. I have talked about shy children who have physical symptoms when interacting with others, who worry excessively, and who, like Hunter, generally avoid social situations that may even include school. Hopefully you have seen that shyness can be a serious problem that needs to be addressed. In these next few chapters, I discuss specific methods to help your overly shy child become more social and confident around others.

You might be surprised to learn that some of the methods in this book have more to do with *you* and *your child's teachers*. This chapter concentrates primarily on what *you* can do as your child practices social and performance situations with and before others. Please remember that you must continually encourage your child to be social with others. *Your child looks to you as a main source of comfort and guidance, so the amount of effort you put into these suggestions relates directly to how successful your child will be.* The methods in this chapter must also be done with *consistency*. You and your partner must work together with your child on an ongoing basis—and likely throughout her childhood—to increase her social behavior and confidence in social and performance situations.

This chapter also contains suggestions for how school officials, working with you, can encourage your child to speak to others more and participate more enthusiastically in group activities. *If you do not have good relationships with officials from your child's school—such as regular and specialized teachers, a guidance counselor, and the principal—begin to develop these relationships now. If you already have good relationships with officials from your child's school, then be sure to maintain these relationships.* This can involve having regular conversations with people most familiar with your child, scheduling meetings to discuss your child's progress, and listening to recommendations from school officials with respect to your child's social and academic status at school.

Many of the recommendations in this chapter involve rewards for positive, social behavior and withdrawal of rewards for inappropriate behavior. Suggestions are also provided for how you and your child's teachers can communicate to your child effectively. You will be asked to provide brief and clear instructions to your child and refrain from inadvertent rewards of avoidant or nonsocial behavior. Helping a child develop more social skill and decrease excessive shyness is a process that requires effort on everyone's part—a child, her parents, teachers, and other school officials. The process may even require help from significant others such as extended family members, peers and classmates, friends, and dating partners.

This chapter also provides you with a glimpse of some of the methods you and your child must develop to reduce excessive shyness. As I discuss parent and teacher strategies, examples are provided that include material from Chapters 4–6. These chapters will also include "flashbacks" to this chapter to illustrate how you can help your child move toward greater social independence. In Chapters 4–6, methods are described for independently practicing social and performance situations while learning to control anxiety in those situations and for developing social skills to increase confidence in these situations. In the next section, I discuss rewarding your child for working to overcome excessive shyness.

Rewarding Your Child for Overcoming Excessive Shyness

Many of the methods in this book require great effort on your child's part. These methods include strategies to help your child relax in difficult situations, change worrisome thoughts toward those that are more realistic, and practice important social skills. One of the toughest assignments your child will receive, however, will be to independently practice social and performance situations that are difficult for her. This may involve walking into a classroom full of people, speaking before others, developing a conversation with someone new, or calling someone on the telephone. Hunter, for example, will need to speak to others to try to develop friendships and become more involved in extracurricular activities.

As your child practices these tasks, reactions from you and from school officials are *very important*. You must reward your child for doing tasks that are difficult for him, though he will obviously begin with less difficult tasks and work his way forward. Let's look at an example:

> Brandon is a 15-year-old boy in tenth grade with trouble speaking before and with others. He is well-behaved and does fine in school but has no friends and speaks only softly to others. His parents and sister complain they often have to ask Brandon to speak up or repeat statements because they did not understand what he said. Brandon's teachers report the same problem and believe that he does not have much self-confidence around others. Brandon does do better communicating to others, especially his parents, when they specifically ask him to repeat statements in a certain way.

Brandon has great trouble speaking to others and likely does not speak very well. A bright spot, however, is that Brandon's parents say their son is receptive to feedback about his speech and does improve his behavior. So, this is a good starting point. We might develop a list of tasks Brandon would have to practice over time. These tasks would be arranged in order from least to most difficult. This list might look something like the following:

1. Speaking publicly to others in a group setting at school (most difficult).
2. Speaking before people Brandon knows somewhat well, such as extended family members.
3. Speaking one-on-one with a peer or adult at school.
4. Speaking to a stranger, such as a clerk in a department store.
5. Speaking on the telephone with a peer.
6. Answering the door at home to speak with a stranger.
7. Speaking clearly to a well-known family member (least difficult).

We would start at the bottom and work our way up for Brandon. Brandon would be asked first to practice speaking to other people in his home in a clear and distinct way. This might involve specific things such as increasing voice volume, establishing eye contact with whoever is listening, speaking articulately (each word pronounced very clearly), and smiling. Of course, many other aspects of speech could be practiced as well and these are covered at greater length in Chapters 4–6.

The first step in helping Brandon might be to have him practice these aspects of speech in *everyday interactions* with his parents and sister. Such practice could occur when Brandon asks for help, makes a request, answers a question, or just talks about his day at school during dinner. As Brandon speaks, his parents and sister can provide feedback to him about his speech and praise him for speaking well. They may also gently urge him to provide more information than simple one-word answers. Consider the following interaction at the family dinner table:

     Mom: Brandon, tell us about your day at school.

    Brandon: (speaking very softly, with head down) It was okay … fine.

      Dad: I'm glad your day went fine, Brandon, could you look up a little when you speak?

    Brandon: (looking up) The day was fine. (Dad smiles at Brandon).

     Sister: Hey, Brandon, what did you think of that fire drill today? I thought it was pretty wild, nobody seemed to know what to do!

    Brandon: (looking at his sister) Yeah, it was pretty funny, people were going off in different directions. I was a little nervous about it but found my way out eventually.

Mom: Wow, that sounds like quite a day.

Brandon: (head up but still speaking softly) Yeah, and then after-ward we all went back to math class, but there wasn't much time to do anything.

Mom: Speak up a little, Brandon, thanks.

Brandon: Okay (speaking a bit louder). At least I got out of having to do math homework today! (Everyone at the table laughs at the joke, reinforcing Brandon for speaking well).

You can see that everyone *gently* nudged Brandon to engage in better speech but did not badger him to do so. His parents did not constantly barrage him with questions, which can irritate a teenager. Brandon's parents and sister instead used subtle and gentle remarks to get Brandon to speak more clearly and then rewarded his speech using smiles and laughter. Of course, you may also use direct rewards such as telling your child how much you enjoy hearing his voice or that you are proud he is working so hard to speak more clearly and directly. You do not have to do this each time your child speaks clearly, but sprinkle in smiles and positive comments every once in a while to motivate your child.

Keep in mind that your child's progress may be a bit slow at first. Remember that he is learning new skills and that he is doing things that are difficult for him to do. Be patient. Imagine your child was first learning to play a complicated piano piece or skateboarding down a sidewalk or think about when he started riding his bicycle. No one can do these things the first time—it takes much practice and, let's face it, some struggles will happen before improvement occurs. *When your overly shy child is learning to speak to others clearly and directly, this is also a new skill that needs a lot of practice*. When frustrations occur, and they will, be sure to let your child know this is expected and that you are proud of his efforts. Also be sure to tell him that continued practice will make things go much easier.

As Brandon does well at easier stages, he can then be asked to prac-tice tasks during more difficult stages. From the list presented above, Brandon would be asked next to answer the door at home and speak on the telephone with a peer. Each of these tasks could be supervised by a parent at a distance so Brandon does not feel "smothered" during the process. Again, these tasks can be built into everyday situations. The doorbell could ring on a Saturday afternoon and Brandon could answer the door and speak to whoever is there. In doing so, he would be expected to make eye contact, speak clearly, ask questions, and receive information. He might be expected as well to handle a situation that is not completely clear. The person at the door might be trying to sell something. In this case, Brandon might be expected to take the person's name and number or ask his parents to handle the interaction.

If Brandon does well in this situation, then his parents should praise his efforts. If Brandon struggled, then his parents could give him feedback about what he could have done differently. Again, this could involve things such as increasing voice volume or responding assertively to the salesperson's pushiness. Brandon's parents would not hover over their son in this situation but might be nearby or within earshot to quietly supervise what was happening and, of course, ensure that nothing dangerous occurred.

As your child starts to practice more complicated social and performance situations, other people will have to become involved in the process. If you review Brandon's list, you see he will eventually be expected to talk with people in community settings and at school. As your child starts these more public practices of social behavior, she will need to be rewarded by people close to the situation. You must develop good relationships with school officials who can help with this process.

Of particular importance will be your child's teachers, guidance counselor, dean, principal, school psychologist, school-based social worker, and specialists such as the school librarian or physical education teacher. These people can quietly supervise your child's social and performance behavior and provide praise and feedback as needed. *But everyone needs to be on the same page.* As you develop a plan for your child to increase her social and performance behavior, you must coordinate this plan with school officials who know what to look for and who can set up practices for your child. This is covered in more detail in a later section and in Chapter 4.

Encouraging Your Child to Interact with Others and Perform Before Others

Another thing you can do on a daily basis with your overly shy child is to encourage her to interact with others and perform before others spontaneously. This means taking advantage of situations during the day that occur unexpectedly and using them to help your child overcome excessive shyness. This strategy is particularly useful for youths who do not respond well to constant questions and prods to be more social. Some children do better in more spontaneous situations, and you can use these situations to teach appropriate social and performance behaviors and reward your child for being less shy (see Box 3.1).

Box 3.1 What rewards to use?

This chapter focused on subtle rewards for a child's social and performance behavior – praise, smiling, jokes, and compliments, for example. These rewards should be used daily to encourage social and performance behavior but might be given with other rewards in some cases. Some tasks a shy child will be asked to do will be quite difficult for her. Examples include starting a conversation with a stranger or peer at school, speaking publicly before others, or attending gym class.

For difficult tasks, subtle rewards such as praise might have to be supplemented with stronger, more tangible rewards. Tangible rewards might include later bedtime, a special dessert, extra time with family members, or movie tickets or another item of monetary value. *The best tangible rewards are those that support social behavior and not solitary or avoidant behavior.* Allowing a child to spend extra time with friends is a good choice but purchasing a videogame or allowing more solitary computer time is not. Link your child's reward with an expectation for social behavior. A child might be given movie tickets, for example, only if he calls a friend to join him. In this way, social behaviors are always practiced.

As your child practices and becomes better at social and performance situations, these situations will hopefully become *self-rewarding.* If your child is expected to ask someone to join him at the movies, for example, the evening will hopefully be enjoyable enough that your child will want to do it again. In similar fashion, the more your child practices calling people on the telephone or asking others in school what their plans are for the weekend, the more rewarding these behaviors will become. Of course, you can still praise and hug your child for his accomplishments along the way!

Let's discuss some examples. Say you are driving your child to school and you stop at a light and see two people talking to each other on the corner. Consider the following conversation with your child:

> *You*: Look at those people on the corner, I wonder what they might be talking about? The one seems to be smiling a lot. I wonder what the other person said to make her smile?
>
> *Your child*: I don't know, maybe her friend told a joke.
>
> *You*: Yes, I think that's a good guess! I'll bet that's what happened. And look how they look at each other when they talk.
>
> *Your child*: What do you mean?
>
> *You*: Well, they seem to be looking at each other when they speak, do you see that?
>
> *Your child*: Well, yeah.
>
> *You*: They are making good eye contact.

In this situation, you have taken a basic life scene and turned it into a learning experience for your child. Even if your child did not respond to you, she is certainly at least thinking about what you said. Riding in a car with your child presents all kinds of opportunities, so turn off the radio and CD/DVD player and find some scenes for discussion. Some people like to play the game of guessing what different people do just by watching them, and this game helps build thinking skills and shows children how others interact. Try this with your child as well. At the park, for example:

> *You*: Okay let's try this one—there's a lady over there with two young children. See? And there is another woman with a couple of children running along and coming toward her.
>
> *Your child*: Okay?
>
> *You*: What do you think is happening there? Who are those two women?
>
> *Your child*: Well, I don't know, but they look kind of tired and they're dressed nice.
>
> *You*: What do you think that means?
>
> *Your child*: Maybe they worked all day and are taking their children to the park.
>
> *You*: Yes, that's a good guess—do you think they know each other?

Your child:	Yeah, it looks like it, the children are talking to each other and going to the slide together. Their mothers are talking and laughing too.
You:	I'll bet they're both schoolteachers—know why?
Your child:	Umm … hmmm … well, one has chalk on her dress and the other has a pencil behind her ear.
You:	You got it! (both laugh).

Other scenes occur during the day that could also serve as a learning experience. Your child could watch someone play a musical instrument before others, see two people argue, or observe a restaurant full of people eating their meal. In each case, ask your child what these people are doing and what they may be thinking so she can get a good idea of normal social behavior. If your child comes up with an unrealistic statement, try to nudge her toward a more realistic one:

Your child:	That waitress just dropped a plate, she's got to be so embarrassed.
You:	Well, she probably is a little embarrassed, but I guess not too much. Do you know why?
Your child:	No.
You:	She's probably dropped a plate before—haven't we all?—but she's still doing her best and being brave by asking for help, don't you think?
Your child:	Yeah, I couldn't do that. I'd be totally embarrassed.
You:	Well, you've been embarrassed before, right?
Your child:	Yeah, I guess.
You:	Well, did your embarrassment last forever?
Your child:	No.
You:	Right, and you were able to handle it, like she is—see?—she's laughing now and already back to work, and no one cares anymore that the plate was dropped (looking around to see everyone resuming their eating and conversing).

In addition to waiting for opportunities to occur, make your own opportunities! Take your child shopping with you and ask her to do things to help you out. These things should generally involve social behavior, such as asking a store clerk for the price of an item, requesting the time from a stranger in the mall, ordering food, and speaking clearly to you as you walk around the shopping center. You certainly do not want to overwhelm your child with tasks to the point that she is upset, but you can sprinkle these requests every so often during the day. If your child did a good job with whatever you asked, then be sure to praise her.

How else do you think you could encourage your child to speak to others or perform before others in some way on a daily basis? Write down some suggestions here for future use:

_____

_____

_____

_____

Working with School Officials to Reward Social Behavior

I mentioned earlier that working with school officials is an important part of helping your shy child. Studies indicate that school-related social and performance situations are the ones with which children have the most trouble. Examples include giving oral reports, writing on the blackboard, speaking with peers and adults at school, going to gym class, eating in a large cafeteria, entering a full classroom, and even using a public restroom (see Worksheet 2.1 from Chapter 2 for more examples). As your child is expected to do more of these difficult tasks, you must work with school officials to arrange these opportunities and see that your child is supervised during his practices. School officials can also give you daily information about your child's distress and avoidance of social and performance situations (see Worksheet 2.2 in Chapter 2).

Another important topic of discussion with school officials is the type and number of extracurricular activities in which your child is eligible to participate. If your child becomes active in social groups, he can practice important social and performance skills, make more friends, and become more confident and less shy. Begin by meeting with your child's guidance counselor and obtain a list of extracurricular activities in which your child is eligible. These activities may be academic, social, musical, or athletic in nature, as long as they involve other children and some adult supervision and guidance.

Later that evening, discuss the list with your child and ask him to choose two or three activities he might like to try. Do not be too concerned about the kind of activity he chooses—let him make the choice because his motivation to attend the group will be greater. Do be concerned, however, if your child refuses to choose a group. Review the list and gently encourage your child to select one activity. Focus on possible advantages of each group and what aspects of the group might appeal most to your child. The goal of this process is to have your child attend at least two or three groups over the next few weeks. Even if he chooses just one of these groups to eventually attend, that is fine. The point is to have your child develop a connection with other children his age, practice his social and performance skills, and make friendships that will make going to school a little easier.

If your child attends a school-related group regularly, check in with your child's guidance counselor or the group leader every so often to see how your child is doing. In particular, make sure your child is not simply "going through the motions" when attending a social group. Some children do not actively participate or they stay to the side reading a book so as not to be fully involved. Instead, encourage your child to be a full participant in these activities and discuss with the group leader ways in which your child could be drawn more into group activities (see also Box 3.2).

Of course, school-related activities are not the only ones in which your child may be interested. Community- and church-based groups are good choices as well. Examples include karate, soccer (or any sport in which your child might be interested), or teen groups at church. I like the latter because these are usually wholesome, community-oriented, supportive, low cost activities. Again, your child should attend at least two or three of these community- or church-based activities and keep going to at least one over the next few weeks. In the beginning, you may wish to accompany him to see how everything is going. Over time, however, your child should attend these groups more independently.

Avoiding Common Pitfalls

Reggie is a 9-year-old boy who rarely speaks to anyone outside of family members. He has passed his early grades at school but officials there are more concerned that Reggie's failure or refusal to speak will begin to affect his more advanced assignments such as reading aloud before classmates. In addition, Reggie has not been tested at school regarding his academic ability. Reggie only whispers to his parents in other public situations. He also refuses to speak on the telephone or even talk to family members he does not know well.

Box 3.2 How can I help my shy child adjust to a new school or school for the first time?

Adjusting to new things can be hard for all of us, especially shy children. Shy children sometimes have special problems adjusting to a new school building or starting school for the first time. What can you do to help your shy child during this difficult transition? Some suggestions follow. These suggestions may also be helpful if your child has had previous problems attending school and you are worried that the problems may occur again at the start of the school year:

- Attend all orientation sessions held at your child's school before the start of the school year. Bring your child with you!
- Purchase or secure all necessary school supplies at least 1 week before the start of school.
- With your child, walk around the school so you and he become *very familiar* with the layout of the school. Show your child his classroom(s) as well as the school cafeteria, gymnasium, library, art and music centers, playground, and other relevant areas. Ask and address your child questions regarding his concerns about getting from one place in school to another.
- Arrange for you and your child to meet your child's school guidance counselor and teacher(s). Show your child the location of the main and guidance counselor's offices so he can stop by during the day to ask questions or express concerns.
- Talk to your child about the school bus, including bus number, stops, times, and what to do if he misses the school bus. Practice the routine of getting to the school bus stop near home in the morning and at school in the afternoon.
- About 2 weeks before the start of school, have your child begin the morning routine as if preparing for school (weekdays only). He should rise from bed at a certain early time, wash, eat, dress, brush his teeth, and complete other regular morning activities as if he were going to school that day. That way, going to school the first day will not made more difficult because of unfamiliarity with the morning routine.

- The night before school starts, have a relaxed conversation with your child about last-minute concerns he might have about going to school the next day.
- Plan to make your schedule flexible during your child's first day of school in case he is jittery or takes a while to enter the school building. In a neutral and firm but supportive manner, require your child to go to school.

As you work with your shy child to improve his social and performance skills and behaviors, avoid doing some things that might seem natural to you. Reggie's refusal to speak in social situations has likely led to a point at which his parents and teachers compensate for his behavior, perhaps by speaking for him or giving him passing grades based only on written or nonverbal work. In this section, I discuss some common pitfalls you should avoid as you work with your shy child to increase his social and performance skills.

Do Not "Rescue" Your Child

A common mistake that parents make is to "rescue" their overly shy child in situations in which he feels some distress. None of us likes to see our children struggle, and so it is natural for parents to help their children whenever possible. But sometimes this "help" can actually get in the way of a child learning to do something independently or to practice skills on his own. This pitfall must be avoided.

Imagine an overly shy child who is invited to another child's birthday party. The child may ask his parents not to take him to the party. He may cry, ask to do something with his parents instead, or actively refuse to go. Many parents, and especially parents of overly shy children, are tempted to allow the child to stay home. Parents may do so for several reasons, such as wanting to rescue their child from feeling distressed, feeling guilty about time spent with the child, and fatigue from dealing with such resistance. Parents may also acquiesce to their child's demand to attend the party with him, or the child will stay close to the parent during the party or constantly ask to leave the party early and go home. Many parents agree to these demands as well.

Giving into a child's demands for avoidance or allowing a child to leave a stressful situation early might seem like the best thing to do in the short run. After all, the child's stress and oppositional behavior are reduced and quality time can be spent between the parent and child. In the long run, however, continued avoidance carries a heavy price. The child is not practicing social skills, is not learning to control anxiety in social or performance situations, is not making friends, and is less likely to be asked to attend another party or social event. Over time, the child's lack of social skill or inability to control anxiety may lead to further social withdrawal, alienation from others, and few friendships.

In this situation, a good response is to insist that a child attend the social event. In the beginning, children do not have to participate fully in whatever group events take place, but as time goes on they would be expected to do so. Encourage your child to stay at the party or social event for as long as possible, preferably until the event ends. If possible and if it is safe to do, ask your child to attend these events independently of you. *Avoid rescuing your child from situations in which he might feel some distress.* He will have to practice managing these situations to overcome excessive shyness.

In related fashion, do not "help" your child too much in different situations. Many family members learn to compensate for a shy child's withdrawn behavior in certain ways. Some parents order food or dessert for a child at a restaurant or ice cream parlor even when the child is older and can easily speak for herself. Encourage your child to speak for herself and, if she fails to do so, be prepared to eat even if she does not. Examine different things you may do during the day to "help" your shy child and begin to ask your child to do these things herself (see also Box 3.3).

Do Not Reward Inappropriate Behavior

Parents sometimes fall in the trap of responding or attending to children whenever they misbehave and forget to reward more positive behavior. When children are playing nicely and quietly, a natural reaction for many parents is to *leave them alone*. But this is exactly the time to reward a child by praising her for playing well and not breaking anything! Similarly, we do not want to end up speaking to our children only when they act out for some reason. The same holds true for an overly shy child.

Box 3.3 Safety signals and quick fixes

Many shy children are ingenious at staying on the fringes of social and performance situations. A child may sit at the edge of the school cafeteria nearest the exit so she can bolt when she feels too anxious. A boy may stand around during gym class and not participate too actively. Another child might mouth words as she "sings" in choir. Other kids need something close by when in an anxious situation, such as a water bottle, cell phone (to call parents), or a relative they know well. Another child might get dressed for gym class in a guidance counselor's office instead of the locker room.

Beware of safety signals. Safety signals are "cheating" behaviors that allow a child to avoid full participation in certain situations. Safety signals are "crutches" a child uses to minimize anxiety – the child is simply delaying anxiety and not learning or practicing skills necessary to control anxiety. A child may not ride the school bus unless his cousin is on board. This might seem like a good short-term solution, but problems will occur if the cousin is out sick one day or has to take another bus the next school year. Also, the child may sit next to his cousin and only speak to her instead of other kids on the bus. Eliminate safety signals and encourage your child to act as independently as possible.

Avoid other "quick fixes" such as class schedule or major school changes or a child's unreasonable request for something that will make a social or performance situation easier. These changes do not lead to long-term improvement. Children who have trouble making friends in one school, for example, often have the same problem in another school. Focus your child instead on doing the hard work of developing the skills discussed in this book.

Many shy children constantly pester their parents for various things, especially avoiding places such as a friend's house or even school. Quite frankly, it can be hard to constantly listen to these requests and not be tempted to negotiate something just to end the incessant questions! But resisting this temptation is important. Your child may ask questions or make comments over and over such as the following:

- Do I really have to go to soccer practice?
- Can't I just stay home?

- I don't want to go!
- Can you come with me?
- This is stupid, I'm not going.

If your child pesters you with the same questions and statements over and over, answer or respond once and then do not respond again for a set period of time. If your child says on Sunday afternoon for the fifteenth time, "Do I really have to go to school tomorrow?," simply say "Yes." Your tone should be matter-of-fact and your answer should be as brief as possible. If your child continues to ask similar questions or make similar comments, ignore them completely for at least an hour. During this hour, feel free to respond to your child when he makes positive statements or discusses some other, nonavoidance-related topic. At the end of the hour, answer the question again once and briefly. I recommend a short statement such as "You are going to school tomorrow. End of story." This way, your child knows there is no room for negotiation.

Over time, feel free to gradually extend the time between answers to 90 minutes, 120 minutes, and 150 minutes. This will help decrease the amount of times your child asks the same question or makes the same statement because he is not receiving a reward for his behavior. This process does require some "selective deafness" and stamina on your part, but you can do it! If necessary, get help from someone such as a spouse or older sibling when the constant questioning becomes too taxing.

Brief Commands and Statements

Another pitfall that parents of shy children sometimes fall into is long lectures or negotiating sessions with their child about various things. This can apply to situations in which a child wants to avoid something and so he constantly badgers his parents to stay home. In other cases, however, parents become frustrated with a child's unwillingness to do something, such as attend a sleepover, and try to bargain with the child or even lecture or intimidate the child into going to the activity. Other parents will constantly interrupt their children, use sarcasm or name calling, or berate their children into compliance. These tactics do not work very well, however.

Keep in mind some basic things as you interact with your shy child:

- Tell your child exactly what you want him to do.
- Give short, direct commands.
- Make direct eye contact when speaking to your child or giving him a command.
- Make sure your child can physically do what you are asking.
- Do a task with your child.
- Reward good listening and discourage poor listening.

Tell your child exactly what you want him to do. Say "Pick your clothes up from your bedroom floor and put them in the laundry basket" instead of "Clean your room." *Be very specific when speaking to your child about shy behavior.* Say "I want you to speak with two classmates today" instead of "Talk more to other people." In addition, focus your child on *pursuing positive behaviors* instead of decreasing negative ones. Say "Speak up so the waitress can hear you" instead of "Stop mumbling."

Give short, direct commands. If you want your child to do something, be brief. Use one-step commands such as "Turn off the television" instead of multiple-step commands. Giving your child a series of one-step commands, though a bit taxing, is better than a laundry list of items all at once that he is not likely to remember. The same is generally true when addressing shy behavior. Ask your child to focus on one key task per day, such as speaking to two friends, calling someone to clarify a homework assignment, or smiling and making eye contact with someone new. Do not overload your child with many tasks—this may overwhelm and discourage your child.

Make direct eye contact with your child when speaking to him. Doing so will result in better compliance to commands because you know you are not competing with attention toward a television or computer. Practicing eye contact is also a good way to increase an important social skill in your child. Your child will also see that eye contact is a good way to maintain attention with others and will hopefully lead to even more social behavior!

Make sure your child can physically do what you ask of her. Parents sometimes ask young children to do something they do not understand or cannot physically do. Learning social and performance skills and developing friendships takes time and patience. Do not expect your shy child to develop solid friendships in 2 weeks or speak to others fluently within a month. Do not rush your child. Start slow and pursue what can be done. Of course, you will also want to subtly challenge your child to do a little better socially each day. Striking a balance between pushing too much and pushing too little can sometimes be hard, so be patient with this process.

Feel free to do many tasks with your child. Being social and less shy does not mean a child never spends time with his family. Spending time with family members in social activities is a great start for many overly shy children. Family reunions, church services, block parties, dinner get-togethers, and attendance at sporting events are great ways for children to be involved with other people in addition to their family members. Of course, your child should eventually do some things on his own, but maintaining regular social contact with your child is fine.

Finally, reward good listening and discourage poor listening. Acknowledge your child when he listens to what you asked him to do. Praise this kind of behavior. Conversely, discourage poor listening. Developing good listening skills is a key social behavior and helps increase compliance and reduce family conflict. In addition, listen actively and appropriately to your child when she speaks to you!

Routines

Many overly shy children are anxious and prefer regular routines during the day. Routines mean the day is predictable and somewhat safe, and this is not a bad thing. If a child has to be ready for school by a certain time, needs to be on the school sidewalk at a certain time to be picked up by a parent, and must be in bed by a certain time, these are not bad things. Develop routines so your child can make it to school, finish homework and chores, and get enough sleep.

A downside to routines, however, especially for overly shy children, is that they can become rigid. Some overly shy and anxious children want their parents to pick them up at a certain time after school with no exceptions. One child in my clinic once insisted that her mother pick her up from school at 3:22 p.m. each day. The girl was enormously anxious about bad things happening if her mother was late, and her mother made special arrangements in the afternoon to make sure she was always there at 3:22 p.m. This created a lot of stress for the mother, however, because of the lack of flexibility in the schedule.

In this situation, I asked the mother to start arriving at school anytime between 3:15 and 3:30 p.m. In the meantime, I worked with her daughter to help her control her anxiety and talk to others appropriately as she waited. Sometimes the mother arrived at 3:15, sometimes at 3:30, sometimes at 3:25, and sometimes even at 3:22. If the mother knew she would arrive later than 3:30, her daughter was instructed to keep her cell phone on and sit in the main office of the school to wait safely. At first, the girl's anxiety was quite high, but this declined over time as she realized that nothing terrible would happen. The unpredictable time also allowed her to practice coping skills such as relaxation and social skills (Chapters 5 to 6) when talking to others. The routine was in place but was not so rigid that a small deviation would cause so much distress.

Such flexibility can be built into other daily routines as well. The morning routine of getting ready for school should be fairly well set but flexible enough so that dawdling will not cause a huge delay. Other routines will have to be more set, such as getting ready for dinner or for bed. The main point to remember, however, is not to let your overly shy child dictate what the routine will be. In many cases, a child is dictating a certain routine to control or minimize her anxiety, but life is not always so predictable. Your child must learn to deal with changing circumstances and accept the fact that not everything is under her control.

Do's and Don'ts

Much information was given in this chapter, so here are a few reminders of do's and don'ts on your part:

Do

- Work with your spouse or partner to consistently bring about positive social and performance behaviors in your child.
- Praise your child often for overcoming excessive shyness and practicing good social and performance behaviors.
- Understand that your shy child is learning a new skill and that patience is required.

- Encourage your child to interact with others and perform before others in everyday situations.
- Use everyday life scenes to teach your child about social interactions.
- Work closely with school officials to develop your child's social behavior.
- Develop a list of contact information for key school officials.
- Explore extracurricular school- and community-based activities in which your child can participate.
- Use brief commands and statements with your child and make direct eye contact when speaking with your child.
- Serve as a good role model for social and performance behaviors.

Don't

- Berate or badger your child into speaking with or performing before others.
- Push your child into social and performance situations he is not ready for.
- "Rescue" your child in all stressful situations.
- Allow a child to leave a social event early because she is mildly distressed.
- Help your child compensate for his shyness, such as ordering food for him in a restaurant.
- Reward inappropriate behavior such as constant questions to avoid something.
- Give your child overly long commands or commands he cannot physically do.
- Give multiple-step commands.
- Forget to continue to spend important family time with your child.
- Adhere to rigid routines or those routines insisted on by your child.
- Allow your child to miss school because of shyness.
- Allow safety signals and quick fixes to address your child's shyness.

What Is Next?

Children who are overly shy will rely a lot on family members to help them become less shy. This chapter provided you with different ways of doing so. Please keep in mind that these recommendations must be put into place on a *regular, daily basis.* Your child will have to continually work to change the shy behaviors that led to avoidance and withdrawal from others. In addition, efforts to change shy behaviors must continue for a long period of time and perhaps throughout childhood and adolescence. In the next few chapters, I focus on specific things *your child* can do more independently to become less shy and more active and competent in social and performance situations. Chapter 4 in particular focuses on arranging specific situations in the community and at school to foster your child's social interactions.

4

Independent Practice in Community and School Settings

Kelsey is a 12-year-old girl in seventh grade who has recently been having great difficulty going to school because she feels isolated and alienated from others while there. She shrinks from others when they get close or when they say something to her, and she seems overwhelmed by new peers and teachers and complex types of assignments at her middle school. Kelsey has always been a bit shy but the stress of entering seventh grade has caused her to withdraw from others even more. She has recently done what she can to stay home and has thus missed several days of school in the past 3 weeks.

Harpreet is a 7-year-old girl in second grade who has never spoken outside her home. She speaks well to her parents and siblings at home but will not speak in community settings such as parks, malls, restaurants, or supermarkets. Harpreet also will not speak to anyone at school, including teachers, other school officials, classmates, and friends. She tends to stay by herself, though she will play nonverbally with other children at times. Her unwillingness to speak at school, however, has led to academic problems because she refuses to read before others or work on group projects in class that require verbal interactions with other children.

This chapter will cover the following topics:

- Establishing a hierarchy of social or evaluative situations that your child must practice.
- Expecting your child to independently interact with others and perform before others.

- Working with your child to increase audible speech in public situations.
- Working with school officials to help you with the tasks described in this chapter.
- Avoiding common pitfalls as your child speaks more in public situations.

Recall from Chapter 3 that you can do many things as a parent to help your child become less shy and more interactive with others. Many of these things involved informal or everyday kinds of actions such as encouraging your child to speak at the dinner table, asking him to answer the door or telephone when necessary, and having discussions about what other people might be thinking and doing. Many of these actions, however, involve a "protected" environment in which your child does things at home or under your very close supervision. In this chapter, I discuss how to help children such as Kelsey interact with others more independently in community and school situations. *Your overly shy child must practice various social and evaluative situations on his own to manage anxiety, develop friendships and social skills, and feel more confident and comfortable in these situations.*

I also discuss ways to help children such as Harpreet who have aspects of *selective mutism* or an unwillingness to speak to others outside the home. Recall from Chapter 1 that selective mutism is, in some cases, an extreme form of shyness or social anxiety that can lead to serious problems such as academic deficiency, lack of friendships, and sadness. Addressing a child who will not speak in school or other public situations can be difficult but not impossible. I have seen many children who are unwilling to speak to others and have successfully helped them overcome their mutism. Many methods for overly shy children also apply to children with aspects of selective mutism.

This chapter is divided into several stages of independent practice. The *first stage* of independent practice is to develop a hierarchy of social and evaluative situations in which your overly shy child has difficulty. This list will help you and your child understand the situations on which to concentrate and the situations your child will be expected to practice. The *second stage* of independent practice involves having your child accomplish specific tasks within these situations. Examples include introducing himself, starting or maintaining a conversation, speaking audibly, and using good social skills such as eye contact, manners, and appropriate emotion. The *third stage* of independent practice is to work with school officials to ensure your child is indeed practicing these actions in class, on the playground, and in other school-based settings. School settings are often the most difficult places for overly shy children and children with selective mutism, so considerable discussion with school officials is often necessary. Let's begin with the first stage, the hierarchy process.

Developing a Hierarchy

A *hierarchy* is a list of social or evaluative situations that range from least to most difficult for your child. These situations will likely involve those in the community as well as those at school. In fact, we may want *two hierarchies* regarding each set of places because overly shy children are often more willing to speak and interact with others in community than in school settings. This is true for children with aspects of selective mutism as well. Your child will likely start with community settings first, but this will serve as an introduction to the more difficult school-based practices she will do later.

Hierarchies usually involve places or specific situations, but can also involve *levels of speaking* such as mouthing, whispering, speaking softly, and speaking in normal tone. Mouthing means a child uses his mouth to form words but no voice is used. The next step is whispering, or saying something very quietly in someone's ear. Whispering can then be transformed into speaking softly and then speaking in a normal tone such that everyone around the child can hear him. Some overly shy children need to practice various levels of speaking in different situations before moving to a more difficult task. Kelsey, for example, may need to speak softly to her teacher before she can speak in a way that others can hear. This is fine as long as Kelsey understands that she must eventually speak clearly and audibly to her teacher and others in class.

Let's form a hierarchy for your child. I recommend having a detailed discussion with your overly shy child about community and school situations that are difficult for him socially. You may wish to consider the strategies we discussed in Chapter 2 to identify these situations, and to draw from Worksheet 2.1. Identify about 5–15 situations and be as specific as possible. For example, your child might say "I have trouble talking to people at school," but narrow this down more specifically to something such as "I don't talk to anyone when I eat lunch in the cafeteria."

The more specific you and your child can be, the more detailed your hierarchy will be and the more effective the methods in this book will be. You and your child could develop less than 5 or more than 15 situations, but stay below 20 to keep the process manageable.

I outline some specific examples of hierarchy items for community and school settings in Tables 4.1 and 4.2. Some of these items include those discussed in Chapter 2. These are not exhaustive lists but they cover the major areas on which I typically focus when addressing overly shy children or those with selective mutism. I recognize that other situations may be specific to your child, so include these as well on your hierarchy.

Get specific information from your child about these items so they can be ranked. *Ask your child to rate on a 0–10 scale the level of distress he feels in each situation as well as how much he wants to avoid that situation.* Recall from Chapter 2 the following ratings: 0 = none, 5 = moderate, and 10 = extreme. Use any number from 0 to 10. No items with distress *and* avoidance ratings of zero should be on the hierarchy. If your child has no distress in a given situation *and* never avoids that situation, then we do not have to address the situation. We will focus only on those situations in which your child has at least some distress and/or avoidance.

Let me illustrate two examples of hierarchies based on Kelsey and Harpreet. Kelsey's sample hierarchy is given in Figure 4.1. Recall that Kelsey was having great trouble adjusting to middle school and was quite withdrawn from teachers and peers. She may have had some shyness in community settings, but for illustrative purposes I concentrate on school situations here. You can see that Kelsey generally found it easier to respond to other people than to initiate conversations. Lower items on her hierarchy, for example, included answering a question from the teacher in class and saying hello to someone who says hello first. Speaking to other people, even if briefly, is part of many of the middle items on her hierarchy. Speaking to other people for longer periods of time, especially when her input about some topic is needed, created considerable distress for Kelsey and so these items are at the top of her hierarchy (most difficult). She dreaded giving an oral presentation to everyone in her class and skipped classes in which she was expected to do so.

You can see that Kelsey's hierarchy contains 15 items, which is manageable. Each item has a distress rating and an avoidance rating, which helps order the items from those less difficult (lower on the hierarchy) to those more difficult (higher on the hierarchy). You do not

Table 4.1 Examples of community settings for a hierarchy

Community settings

Answering a question during Sunday school class

Asking a stranger in a public place for the time or for directions

Asking someone out on a date

Being assertive with someone

Being introduced to new people

Expressing an opinion to other people

Going to a party or a similar social gathering

Going to an extracurricular activity

Greeting others (known and unknown) at church

Inviting a friend to do an activity

Speaking to several potential friends (unknown peers) at soccer practice or a birthday party or other social event

Speaking to one potential friend (unknown peer) at soccer practice or a birthday party or other social event

Speaking to potential friends (unknown peers) at a park

Speaking to friends at soccer practice or a birthday party or other social event

Speaking to other adults in public situations

Speaking to parents and siblings at the mall

Speaking to parents and siblings at church

Speaking to neighborhood friends at a park

Speaking to neighborhood friends in one's driveway

Speaking to parents in a public place such as a market

Using one word to order ice cream for a clerk

Using 2-3 sentences to order food for a waiter or clerk

have to use these ratings, but many children find it helpful and fun to order items in this way. As we begin independent practice with Kelsey, we will do so with the lower items on the hierarchy and gradually progress toward the higher items. Each of these items may be divided as necessary. Kelsey may find, for example, that speaking to two peers

Table 4.2 Examples of school settings for a hierarchy

School settings

Answering a question in class

Asking the teacher a question in class

Attending physical education class

Eating in the school cafeteria

Participating in a group or team project at school

Playing a musical instrument or singing before others

Playing with peers on the playground

Reading aloud to classmates and the teacher or engaging in show-and-tell

Speaking to others as appropriate during academic activities

Speaking to staff members at school

Speaking to parents at school

Speaking to the teacher in the classroom, such as asking for help or answering a question

Speaking to peers in the classroom during small group activities or during free time

Speaking to peers in hallways and related situations

Speaking to peers in the classroom

Speaking to peers at lunch/cafeteria

Speaking to peers on the playground

Speaking to peers on the school bus

Speaking to a school official in his/her office

Speaking to others in a classroom with classmates present plus the teacher

Speaking to others in a classroom with ten classmates present plus the teacher

Speaking to others in a classroom with five classmates present plus the teacher

Speaking to others in a classroom with two friends and the teacher sitting at his/her desk

Speaking to others in a classroom with two friends on the other side of the room

Continued

Table 4.2 cont'd

Speaking to others in an empty classroom

Speaking to others in the cafeteria with others present

Speaking to others in an empty school cafeteria

Speaking to others in the library with others present

Speaking to others in an empty school library

Speaking to teachers in the classroom

Speaking to teachers on the playground at school

Taking a test

Using the restroom at school

Walking in the hallway at school

Writing on the blackboard in class

---

in the school cafeteria is too difficult. Instead, she could try to speak to just one person and then progress to speaking to two people.

Harpreet has aspects of selective mutism, and many of these children need a detailed hierarchy for community situations before focusing on school situations. A sample hierarchy for Harpreet that contains community items is given in Figure 4.2. You can see that her hierarchy is structured similarly to Kelsey's for illustrative purposes. However, many

Situations	Distress Rating	Avoidance Rating
1. Reading or speaking aloud to all peers in class	10	10
2. Working on a group project in class	9	9
3. Introducing oneself to someone not well known	8	9
4. Maintaining a conversation with someone not well known	8	8
5. Maintaining a conversation with someone fairly well known	7	8
6. Speaking to the guidance counselor at school	7	7
7. Asking the teacher a question in class	6	6
8. Writing on the blackboard in class	6	5
9. Speaking to 1-2 peers in the school cafeteria	4	4
10. Speaking to anyone in the hallway at school	3	4
11. Speaking to 1-2 peers in physical education class	4	3
12. Speaking to 1-2 peers in regular class	3	3
13. Speaking to 1-2 classmates on the school bus	3	2
14. Saying hello to someone who says hello first	2	2
15. Answering a question from the teacher in class	1	1

Figure 4.1. Sample hierarchy for Kelsey's school settings.

Situations	Distress Rating	Avoidance Rating
1. Asking someone not known for the time or for directions	10	10
2. Saying 2-3 sentences to someone not known at church	9	9
3. Saying 2-3 sentences to someone known at church	8	9
4. Saying 2-3 sentences to a friend outside the home	8	8
5. Saying hello to someone not known at a mall	7	8
6. Saying hello to someone not known at a park	7	7
7. Saying hello to someone at soccer practice	6	6
8. Saying hello to someone at a birthday party	6	5
9. Speaking to a friend at the park	4	4
10. Speaking to a friend in one's driveway	3	4
11. Saying hello to someone not known at church	4	3
12. Saying hello to someone known at church	3	3
13. Using a sentence to order food from a waiter	3	2
14. Using one word to order ice cream from a clerk	2	2
15. Speaking to parents in a public place such as a market	1	1

Figure 4.2. Sample hierarchy for Harpreet's community settings.

children such as Harpreet need very small increments from one item to the next. Progress for these children is measured a little more slowly than for children such as Kelsey. You can see that small advances are part of Harpreet's hierarchy. For example, she might say two or three sentences to someone known at church and then say two or three sentences to someone not known at church.

Harpreet's hierarchy also begins (at the bottom) with easier items that include speaking to people she knows well in public situations. Many of her easier items are a bit closer to home or involve situations in which she is familiar, such as a local park or restaurant or church. Higher items on her hierarchy require a bit more independent speech, but all of her items will be under the careful supervision of a parent (safety first!). Once Harpreet has mastered the items on this hierarchy, another hierarchy could be developed for other community situations or for school situations. You do not have to limit the number or type of hierarchies you want to develop.

Children such as Harpreet sometimes need another hierarchy that accompanies the one in Figure 4.2. Figure 4.3 represents a mini-hierarchy of ways that Harpreet can communicate to someone during each item of her main hierarchy (Fig. 4.2). The hierarchy in Figure 4.3 simply ranges from less to more difficult (formal ratings are not necessary). Let's take an item from Figure 4.2 as an example: speaking to a friend

	More difficult
1. Speaking audibly and clearly all words to someone	↑
2. Speaking audibly and clearly most words to someone	↑
3. Speaking audibly and clearly 1-2 words to someone	↑
4. Speaking softly all words to someone	↑
5. Speaking softly most words to someone	↑
6. Speaking softly 1-2 words to someone	↑
7. Whispering all words to someone	↑
8. Whispering most words to someone	↑
9. Whispering 1-2 words to someone	↑
10. Whispering to others in the presence of someone	↑
11. Communicating vocally but not verbally, such as grunting, making high-pitched sounds, or using incomplete words such as "eh" for yes and "un" for no	↑ ↑ ↑
12. Communicating nonverbally but using one's mouth, such as mouthing words or phrases such as "hello" or "please"	↑ ↑
13. Communicating nonverbally or without using one's mouth (e.g., writing words in the air, pointing, gesturing)	↑ ↑
14. Communicating by writing or drawing on paper	↑
	Less difficult

Figure 4.3. Sample mini-hierarchy for Harpreet's speaking behavior to someone.

at a park. In this situation, formal speech may not be possible right away, but we could ask Harpreet to do some things in Figure 4.3 as a start (be sure the friend is patient). Harpreet could be asked to mouth the word hello to her friend and then go play as a reward. The next time she could be asked to whisper hello to her friend or even say hello softly. As Harpreet practices this item on her hierarchy, she will hopefully become more comfortable with speech and eventually say hello quite audibly to her friend.

A special note regarding children with aspects of selective mutism such as Harpreet: you may need to begin the hierarchy and practice process at home rather than in community or school settings. A home-based hierarchy might include items such as speaking to you or siblings, speaking to visitors your child knows well, speaking to visitors your child does not know well, speaking to peers inside the home with or without the parents present, talking on the telephone with a friend or familiar relative, talking on the telephone with an unfamiliar person, and answering the door or telephone. All of these should be accomplished *before* you consider asking your child to speak in public. Be sure that your child gradually speaks more audibly in these home-based situations.

Your child may begin by mouthing words, then whispering, then speaking softly, and then speaking more audibly.

Hierarchies are meant to be fluid, meaning they can change. If you develop a hierarchy with your child, do not be surprised if she tells you later that one item should be ranked higher or lower than before. As children become more comfortable practicing their communication with others, they often progress quickly. Keep in mind, however, that your child could also get "stuck" at one of her hierarchy items and may need considerable practice, or the item may need to be pulled apart a bit for your child to progress. I recommend having conversations with your child every two or three days about his hierarchy and whether any changes need to be made.

Independent Practice in Community Settings

Once your hierarchies have been developed, and your child with excessive shyness or selective mutism is speaking well within the home, then independent practice in community settings can begin. This can flow naturally from the home-based ideas discussed in Chapter 3. Your child will begin to practice speaking well to others in public situations, but you will be there to give feedback, to prompt him to speak more clearly, and to provide support. As your child progresses, he will hopefully do many social tasks on his own. You may feel uneasy about gently pushing your child to do more independent practice, but keep in mind that the overall goal is to help your child be more effective in social situations, develop friendships, and feel more comfortable and confident when speaking to others. Let's discuss community practices in three stages.

First Stage of Community Practice

The first stage of your child's independent practice may involve community-based situations *that are close to your home*. I am assuming at this point that your child speaks well at home and with different people in his home. If this is not the case, then help your child establish good interactions with others in his home before he tries to do so in community settings. Some children need considerable practice speaking well to others within a comfortable setting such as their kitchen, and that is fine. I am also assuming that easier or lower items on your child's hierarchy involve some of these close-to-home practices. If your child can already do the things I am about to discuss, then you and he can jump ahead a bit.

Your child's first community practices may include his backyard, courtyard, driveway, or even a few steps from his front door. Under your supervision, ask your child to speak to a neighborhood friend, the mail carrier, or someone he sees on a regular basis. Your child can practice saying hello or some light conversation if he is comfortable doing so. As he practices, give him feedback about his speech and volume, eye contact, and topic of conversation. If your child does not know what to say, help him by suggesting he discuss the weather, a new toy, a pet, or some topic about which he likes to talk. As your child does this initial practice, he can continue to do home-based things such as answer the door or telephone and talk with visiting relatives.

Keep in mind that later chapters in this book discuss methods to help your child develop good social skills (Chapter 5), manage physical feelings of distress (Chapter 6), and change worrisome thoughts during social interactions (Chapter 6). You may wish to review and start these methods at this point in your child's independent practice to help him develop his skills and control anxiety. The most important method in this book, however, is *constant practice* with helpful feedback from you, teachers, and peers.

Once your child can speak well and audibly to others near his home, more demanding community items from her hierarchy can be addressed next. Recall that Harpreet's first community practices involved speaking to her parents in a public place such as a supermarket. I recommend that you take your child with you to places you regularly visit in your neighborhood, such as the market, post office, or convenience store. Go whenever you would normally do so, such as shopping for groceries on a Saturday morning.

Tell your child in advance that he is expected to say at least one word to you in the market. The word can be any word he chooses, but it must be audible. If your child can already do this, then increase your expectations. You may ask your child to say hello to the greeter at the store, to ask a clerk where a certain item is located, or have a conversation with you that others could overhear. Your child should do whatever task you decide within the normal shopping time. Do not give him special time extensions such as lingering in the store longer than you normally would. Praise your child for doing what you asked him to do and give him feedback on how well (or not so well) he did. *Always praise effort.* If your child hesitates about speaking in this public place, then prompt him gently and remind him what is expected of him. Patience is a virtue in these situations. Your child may need several trips to the market, for example, before he can speak to a clerk.

Second Stage of Community Practice

The second stage of independent community practice will generally involve situations in which your child is less familiar. Recall from Harpreet's hierarchy, for example, that some of her items included saying hello to someone she does not know at church, speaking to a waiter or clerk to order food, and talking to someone at a birthday party. These practices will generally involve less supervision on your part. You may be nearby, but not so close that you are hovering or able to give immediate feedback. These situations are often the first that your child practices much more independently. Be sure your child does not try these tasks until he is interacting well with others during home-based situations *and* community situations discussed in the first stage.

As before, tell your child specifically what you want him to do. Avoid vague statements such as "talk to that boy" and instead use statements such as "walk up to that boy and say hello so he can hear you." Remain nonchalant, neutral, and matter-of-fact in your demeanor. Your child may have some difficulty approaching someone, so use encouraging but firm statements such as "You can do it," "You know what you need to do," or "You need to use your words." Ignore non-compliant behaviors or complaints about what you are asking your child to do. Do not criticize or lecture your child. Instead, adopt a supportive and hopeful tone and continue to prompt your child to practice his social task. Many overly shy children eventually do what is asked of them when parents remain firm and gently insist that they practice their assigned task.

Some practices in this stage can involve natural consequences for speaking or not speaking appropriately. For example, you could take your family to an ice cream parlor and tell everyone that whoever verbally orders ice cream receives ice cream. Your child may be expected, depending on his hierarchy item, to say one word such as "cone" or "bowl" or "chocolate." However, he may also be at the point at which he is expected to use a complete sentence such as "I would like a chocolate cone, please." *The important point to convey to your child is that speaking will result in ice cream and that no speaking will result in no ice cream.* Do this practice *only* if you feel you can follow through with the negative consequence if your child does not speak. Your child may need several tries to speak successfully, and that is fine. If your family is enjoying ice cream and your child decides to order at the end of the trip, then allow him to do so. Always praise effort as well as success.

Other community practices at this stage include speaking to people your child does and does not know well in situations such as parks, malls, restaurants, and sporting activities. Your child should continue to receive feedback from you and others about how she did, practice good social skills (Chapter 5), and practice methods to reduce anxiety (Chapter 6). Remember to split a hierarchy item if your child has great difficulty. Keep in mind that this stage can take several weeks or months, and that more practice will speed things along.

Third Stage of Community Practice

The third and final stage of independent community practice involves difficult items near the top of your child's hierarchy. These more difficult items may include more extended conversations with people in a wider variety of settings. These items may also involve doing things your child has never done before, such as asking a stranger (under your supervision) for directions or for the time. They should also involve greater independence, more discussions with less familiar people, and speaking to others with more people around. Try to make these difficult tasks as natural as possible. If your child regularly attends church with you, for example, then meeting and greeting people before and after the service may be a good idea.

Give your child some suggestions as to what he can say before he speaks to someone. Your child will hopefully be able to do this more independently with practice, but providing some early help is okay. Your child should always be prepared for different social situations by knowing what he can say and knowing how he should say it (see Chapter 5 for social skills help). Help your child practice saying hello, asking questions, and speaking so others can hear.

Some of these more difficult community practices can set the stage for the school-based practices to be discussed next. For example, your child could begin to ask and answer questions in Sunday school class, which may mimic what he will need to do in regular school. Your child could also initiate conversations with others as appropriate, speak using several sentences, and speak before larger numbers of people. Your child could, for example, introduce himself to a new neighborhood friend, carry on an extended conversation with her private music teacher, and talk about a soccer play with his teammates. I have found that a child's success in each of these steps eases school-based practices, which are described next.

Independent Practice in School Settings

Once your overly shy child is speaking well to others at home *and* in various community settings, then she should practice in school settings. I usually recommend that school settings be the last place to practice because these situations tend to be the most difficult, but it does not have to be this way. Some children like to work on community and school settings at the same time, which is fine. Other children prefer starting at school and then moving to community settings to practice, which is also fine. Let's talk about some stages of independent practice in school settings.

First Stage of School Practice

If your overly shy child has great difficulty speaking to others at school, as Kelsey did, then be sure she begins her independent practice in *low-key situations*. Low-key situations at school might involve speaking to one or two people your child knows well, speaking to a trusted teacher in an empty classroom, speaking to others on the playground, speaking to a guidance counselor in her office, or speaking to others immediately before or immediately after school. Other children find it easier to interact with peers at a school bus loading area or in an area near but not on the school campus, and some children find it easier to speak with just a few people when not many others are around. Some children like to begin speaking to others at the school playground on weekends because school is not in session. Explore with your child how he would like to start his independent practice at school by focusing on these low-key situations.

Your child's independent practice at this stage will likely involve less direct supervision from you. The more your child practices independently, the less immediate input he will receive from you. You will therefore want to work closely with helpful school officials (see later section) who can provide feedback to you about your child's performance or help your child become more social at school. In addition, some of your child's early practices at school may involve speaking to school officials such as teachers, a guidance counselor, a principal, or staff members.

As your child begins these independent practices at school, encourage him to arrive early to class, say hello to more people, and ask questions. Arriving early to class allows for more opportunities to speak to peers. I encourage overly shy children to ask people questions such as "How was your weekend?," "How are you doing?," and "How is school going?" Many overly shy children find it difficult to start conversations, but simple questions such as these are good icebreakers that do not require much work on your child's part. In some cases, the icebreaker question could even lead to a more lengthy conversation, which is what we want to see eventually.

Second Stage of School Practice

Your child's second stage of independent school practice should involve lower- and middle-level items on his hierarchy. Recall Kelsey's school-based hierarchy in Figure 4.1. Her lower-level hierarchy items included situations such as answering a question from the teacher in class, speaking to one or two peers and classmates in different settings at school, and writing on the blackboard in class. These independent practices can follow naturally from the low-key practices discussed in the first stage. For example, speaking to one or two peers or classmates can follow some of the opening questions in the previous paragraph. Or Kelsey could begin to say hello to two or three people in the hallway at school after having practiced saying hello to two or three people in her class.

Your child may also wish to practice some abilities before completing tougher tasks on his hierarchy. If your child is nervous about writing on the blackboard, for example, then have him practice this skill at home. If your child is apprehensive about what to say to people, do a short role play in which you pretend to be another student. If your child has trouble answering a question from a teacher in class, ask the teacher for some sample questions that you could pose to your child at home. This kind of behind-the-scenes work often helps a child feel more confident when faced with the actual task.

Your child's practice at this stage should involve certain key elements:

- Be sure the task is safe and predictable for your child. Saying hello to someone in his class may be easier than trying to say hello to someone two grades above him.
- Be sure your child practices items on his hierarchy *every day*. The frequency with which your child practices relates directly to how much progress he will make.
- Continue to have your child speak to others at home and in community settings as she practices at school. She will quickly gain confidence and skill this way.
- Ask your child to stay in a social situation *as long as possible*. Some overly shy children say hello and then quickly leave a situation, but a better practice involves sustained effort to lengthen conversations, manage anxiety, and develop good social skill. This is especially important if your child finds another child who is willing to have an extended conversation with him.
- Ask your child to use the methods discussed in Chapters 5 and 6 as he practices interacting with others.

Third Stage of School Practice

Your child's third stage of independent school practice should involve the most difficult items on his hierarchy. Recall Kelsey's hierarchy of school-based situations in Figure 4.1. Her most difficult items included maintaining a conversation with someone not well known, introducing herself to people, working on a group project in class, and reading or speaking aloud to all of her peers in class. Kelsey will likely need extended practice in each area to become fully comfortable, but this is doable.

Work with your child *and* with relevant school officials to help your child in these difficult areas. Let's discuss reading aloud to classmates as an example. This task could be divided into several smaller tasks if Kelsey has great difficulty speaking before a large group. One idea is to have Kelsey practice reading a magazine article or book report to her teacher in an empty classroom. As Kelsey does this, her teacher can give her feedback about her voice volume, posture, articulation, and use of time. Kelsey can also practice relaxation and breathing methods (see Chapter 6) to help manage her anxiety.

As Kelsey becomes better at giving her report in this way, the task can gradually become more difficult and closer to the final goal.

For example, Kelsey could be asked to read to her teacher and two of her classmates, then read before 5 other people, then 10 other people, and finally to the entire class. In this way, Kelsey gains more confidence in her ability with each step and eventually reaches her final goal, or the top of her hierarchy.

This kind of gradual approach can be used in other ways as well. For example, your child could first interact with others in a school hallway when few people are around and eventually progress to speaking with more people around. Some overly shy children prefer to speak to others in more secluded settings such as the school library or main office before speaking in class. Always expect more effort from your child over time. Always ask your child for more speech, more audible speech, and speech with more people. Do not push your child so hard that she becomes overly frustrated or upset, but do nudge her to continually practice her social behaviors.

The last stage of practice usually involves situations that may or may not be on your child's hierarchy but that occur naturally during the day. Your child should eventually be at a point at which he can adapt to any social or evaluative situation that arises. For example, someone new might say hello to your child, your child may be asked to do something different in class, or your child must be assertive with someone. Good success is achieved when a child can handle these situations without distress or avoidance and with good skill. Speaking to others should become something your child enjoys and something that comes more naturally to him. Point out to your child that his improved speaking behavior creates positive responses from others.

If your child is not yet at this point, then continue to practice the methods in this book. Practice can take several weeks or months, which is fine. Remember, however, that many shy children continue to show elements of shyness. The final goal is not to change your child into a social butterfly but to simply help him become more confident and comfortable in social situations. Be realistic in your goals.

Working with School Officials

Working with teachers and other school officials is especially important once your child practices social tasks at school. School officials can provide feedback to you and your child about your child's performance in social and evaluative tasks, help your child become more social at school, or serve as items on your child's hierarchy (e.g., speaking to the guidance counselor in her office). Frequent contact with relevant school officials via emails, calls, daily progress reports, and discussions is quite helpful in this regard (see Chapter 2). In addition, speak with school officials about extracurricular activities for which your child is eligible and how he can participate.

If your child is extremely shy or, like Harpreet, will not speak at school, then I recommend a thorough assessment and intervention process that involves several school officials, including a school psychologist or school-based social worker. Some children with intense shyness or selective mutism benefit from a 504 plan that allows for more intense focus on the methods described in this book as well as more formal techniques or academic or language interventions as necessary. A child who will not speak at school, for example, may need special help in academic tasks such as reading aloud or taking standardized tests that require some verbal input. You may wish to consult the following book: C. A. Kearney, *Helping children with selective mutism and their parents: A guide for school-based professionals*, 2010, Oxford University Press.

Avoiding Pitfalls When Working with Your Child

You and your child will be working hard during the practices outlined in this chapter. *The biggest mistake* that parents make during this process is *rescuing* their child from a social situation. As parents, we do not like to see our child in distress and thus we have a natural tendency to try to prevent this. As such, some parents allow a child to miss a social obligation when he cries about having to go or allow a child to leave a social gathering early because he feels uncomfortable. Your overly shy child will eventually enjoy social interactions more if he regularly goes to these gatherings and stays there to practice his skills. Serve as a good role model for your child by attending social gatherings yourself.

Another mistake parents sometimes make during these practices is to look for "quick fixes" that allow a child to subtly avoid certain situations. For example, a child may say he will ride the school bus only if his cousin rides with him, and a parent may try to arrange this. Or a child may ask for a table in a restaurant that is near the door so others are not near him. Parents should try not to accommodate these kinds of requests and instead encourage a child to be as independent as possible in social situations.

Other parents naturally become frustrated when they think their child is not progressing fast enough. They may even berate, lecture, or criticize their child during his practices. I cannot say how long it will take for your overly shy child to become more social, but patience for at least several months is a good idea. You will have to find a balance between pushing your child too hard and nudging him too little, which will take some practice on your part. In the meantime, adopt a supportive and helpful tone with your child.

Do's and Don'ts

Here are a few reminders of do's and don'ts on your part:

Do

- Work with your child to develop hierarchies of social and evaluative situations that he can practice at home, in community settings, and at school.
- Reward your child often for practicing good social behaviors in these situations.
- Give your child helpful feedback about his performance in these situations, especially how he speaks to others and how he manages his anxiety.
- Adopt a supportive and helpful tone as your child practices skills in different situations.
- Work closely with school officials to develop your child's social behavior.

Don't

- Rescue your child from all social situations.
- Berate or lecture or criticize your child during his practices.
- Allow quick fixes to address your child's shyness.

What Is Next?

Much of the hard practice we covered in this chapter will be made easier if your child also practices some other skills covered in the next two chapters. The next chapter covers important social skills your child can practice as she interacts with others, and Chapter 6 covers ways to help manage anxiety by relaxing physically and changing worrisome thoughts. Practicing all of these skills together will greatly improve your overly shy child's interactions with others.

5

Improving Social Skills

Ling is an 8-year-old girl in the third grade who is quite shy and awkward around other children at school. She rarely makes eye contact with people, often keeps her head down, and is hard to understand when speaking. Ling speaks very softly and tends to stay by herself during lunch and recess. Her classmates say they like her but do not know her very well. Some of her classmates have invited Ling to play with them but she usually shakes her head and simply walks around the playground. At this point in the school year, most of Ling's classmates are ignoring her and Ling sometimes appears sad.

This chapter will cover the following main topics:

- Learning about social skills in overly shy children.
- Encouraging the development of social skills in an overly shy child.
- Using social skills during independent practices.
- Working with school officials to encourage social skills in an overly shy child.

As overly shy children grow up, they tend to avoid other people, as Ling does. They avoid new situations that can include peers, classmates, or other people they meet. Many of these children also show social behaviors that indicate they do not want to speak to others or that they are unwilling to make an effort to play or interact with others. You can see that Ling keeps her head down, declines requests to play, and skulks around the playground. These behaviors send a certain message to other children: *Leave me alone.* As other children do leave her alone, however, Ling's shyness will only get worse, even if she does want friends.

Parents often say their shy child "has been like this since birth." Many overly shy children have a certain temperament from an early age that leads to solitary behavior for several years (Chapter 2). Ling's parents said their daughter always played by herself at preschool and usually just wanted to be around family members. As this solitary behavior continues, however, there is little chance Ling will interact with others and learn important social skills that guide her interactions with others.

As shy children fail to develop important social skills such as eye contact when speaking, their social interactions with others become more awkward (see Fig. 5.1). Other children had trouble understanding what Ling was saying and perhaps ridiculed her as a result. What do you think these awkward social interactions will lead to for Ling? You guessed it: even more withdrawn behavior, more alienation from peers and others, and even fewer opportunities to practice social skills. This cycle continues over time and can get worse, creating more shyness and perhaps leading to a point at which a child has no friends.

This chapter focuses on important social skills children need to learn to successfully interact with and perform before others. Social skills are skills many people take for granted, such as not interrupting

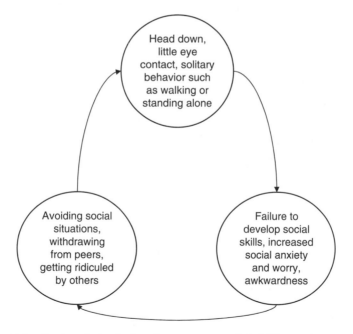

Figure 5.1. Cycle of shy behaviors, poor social skills, and withdrawal.

people when they speak. For some overly shy children, however, there are few opportunities to learn or practice these basic skills. Your child may thus need some help learning how to talk with others and how to make friends. First, though, let's talk about what "social skills" means.

What Are Social Skills?

Social skills are behaviors we use to interact with others and perform before others. Think about having a conversation with a co-worker or partner. What are some important social skills you use during this process? Some of these skills are so basic or second nature to us that we do not think about them much. We make eye contact, we listen as the other person is talking, we do not interrupt, we speak when the other person is finished, we stay about 3–5 feet away from the person to avoid "crowding" her, we ask questions, we give compliments, and we control our emotions when the other person tells us something we may not like to hear!

Reading and digesting a list of all possible social skills would take quite a bit of time and energy, so this chapter focuses on skills most important for social and performance behavior and for making and keeping friends. These key social skills are in Checklist 5.1. Review this list and place a checkmark next to those that seem to be a problem for your child. If necessary, ask others to help you. If you cannot decide whether a particular skill is an issue, ask your child or watch for the skill closely in the next few days. Watch your child to note his reaction when someone tells him something he does not want to hear. Does he have trouble controlling his emotions or refuse to speak, or can he discuss the issue clearly and reasonably?

As you survey this list, keep in mind that *not all shy children necessarily have poor social skills*. You may not place any checkmarks on the list, and that is okay. Shy children usually fall into one of three types with respect to social skills:

- Some shy children have perfectly fine social skills; they simply do not show their skills often enough with others.
- Some shy children have good social skills that could use some fine-tuning; they are a little awkward because they do not practice social skills often, but need only more practice to be fine.
- Some shy children such as Ling do not have good social skills and need considerable work to learn and practice these skills.

Checklist 5.1 Important social skills in children and adolescents

Accepting invitations from others for play or other social interaction

Accepting praise and compliments from others

Answering the door or telephone

Asking others for help or information

Being assertive in saying "no" or when asking for something

Calling someone on the telephone or inviting someone for a fun activity

Controlling impulses and anger instead of acting quickly upon them

Cooperating with others in a game or project

Dealing with sadness or anxiety

Dealing with embarrassing or stressful situations such as teasing

Delaying gratification, such as completing schoolwork before playing or television

Eating appropriately around others

Giving and accepting compliments and affection

Greeting others appropriately, such as saying hello and smiling

Identifying emotions in oneself and others, such as happiness, sadness, and anger

Initiating and maintaining conversations with others

Introducing oneself or other people

Joining activities with peers

Keeping head up when speaking to others

Listening to others appropriately

Maintaining eye contact with others during a conversation

Checklist 5.1 cont'd

Maintaining personal hygiene and grooming

Ordering a meal in a food establishment

Performing athletically before others

Refraining from interrupting or inappropriately touching other people

Refraining from rude behaviors such as yelling, insults, sarcasm, or hitting

Resisting group pressure to do something inappropriate

Resolving conflicts with others, such as reasonably negotiating solutions to problems

Sharing feelings appropriately

Speaking articulately

Speaking in a clear and audible tone of voice

Speaking or reading before others

Taking the perspective of other people, or knowing why others act as they do

Taking turns when playing a game

Using manners such as saying "please," "thank you," and "excuse me"

Writing before others

In which category does your child most closely fit? Watch your child interact with others independently or ask other people what they think. Teachers, babysitters, siblings, and relatives are sometimes good sources of information about this because they see your child interact with others in your absence. Be open-minded as you listen to what people say to you. Bear in mind that children who are not shy must also continue to practice their social skills, so even if your child has good social skills he may need some encouragement to keep practicing (Chapter 3).

Developing Social Skills in a Shy Child

When a child needs help developing social skills, people close to him are going to be very important in this process. Recall from Chapters 3 and 4 the different ways in which parents can generally encourage children to interact with others and perform before others:

- Reward your child for overcoming excessive shyness.
- Practice good speech in everyday situations.
- Engage in daily situations such as answering the door.
- Examine basic life scenes to talk about social interactions.
- Bring your child with you on errands to increase his social behavior.
- Increase his participation in extracurricular activities.
- Design hierarchies and ask your child to independently practice social situations.
- Avoid common pitfalls that inadvertently reward shy behavior.

I next discuss more specific ways to help your child develop social and performance skills such as those listed in Checklist 5.1. Continue to practice the methods in Chapters 3 and 4 to increase opportunities for practicing social skills. A child may develop good social skills with her family members but must also practice these skills outside the home. *A child must interact with many others in a positive and constructive way so she can make and keep friends and find social behavior to be rewarding.*

Identify up to five social skills from Checklist 5.1 that you think are most difficult for your child. If you feel your child has trouble with more skills, or has severe trouble with these skills, then you may wish to seek the help of a qualified mental health professional who specializes in social skills training. If you feel you can identify only one or two skills and not five, that is okay. Recall that some children simply need more practice for certain skills, so we can still work on those that need fine-tuning. The methods in this chapter still apply.

Which social skills from Checklist 5.1 might we choose for Ling? Several skills problems apply to her:

- Making and keeping eye contact with others.
- Keeping her head up when speaking to others.
- Speaking articulately when interacting with others.
- Speaking in an audible tone of voice.
- Accepting invitations from others to play.

Develop the same kind of list for your child, again focusing on a maximum of five main skills for now. Develop your list for your child here:

_____

_____

_____

_____

_____

Arrange these skills in order from those that are somewhat developed and do not need too much practice, or those needing the least amount of work, to those that need considerable practice or the most amount of work. Ling's ordering might be as follows:

- Speaking articulately when interacting with others (needs the most work).
- Accepting invitations from others to play.
- Speaking in an audible tone of voice.
- Keeping her head up when speaking to others.
- Making and maintaining eye contact with others (needs the least work).

Order your list for your child here:

_____ (needs the most work)

_____

_____

_____

_____ (needs the least work)

This list gives you a good place to start social skills training. You and your child will gradually progress through this list by starting at the bottom and working up. *Keep in mind that doing so will require cooperation on your child's part, so including him in this process, and perhaps having him read this chapter, is a good idea.* If your child resists developing his social skills, then reward positive efforts on his part. Most shy children want to make and keep friends but do not know how. Tell your child that developing ways of talking to other people is important and will help him become less shy and alone. You also want to tell him, however, that practicing social skills is something he *must do every day*. The good news is that learning good social skills and putting them into practice does not have to take a long time.

Let's talk next about specific ways to teach social skills to your child. You and your child will initially work together on this process. As your child improves, however, he must practice these skills more independently with peers, classmates, and other children (Chapter 4). The main way to teach social skills to children is to use modeling, practice, and feedback—much of this chapter is spent on this approach. Other suggestions are also made about improving your child's ability to take the perspective of others and to identify emotions in himself and others.

Modeling, Practice, and Feedback

When we learn a new skill for the first time, we often watch how other people do the behavior. Young children who are just learning to speak correctly watch how their parents speak to them and then adjust their speech. A young child might say "uh-eee" for "cookie," and a parent may smile and slowly say "COO-K-IE" so the child understands how to say the word correctly. Or a child who wants to ride a bike may first watch other people put on their helmet, sit on the seat, achieve balance, and push the pedals with their feet. Older children and adolescents copy others as well—they watch what kinds of music their peers download or how others download computer material in the first place!

When children learn by watching others, this is called *modeling*. Modeling is a great way to teach social skills. Children can watch other people talk to one another or perform before others to learn effective ways of communicating or interacting. Many overly shy children, because they often withdraw from social situations, do not often model appropriate social interactions. We have to change this for your child. He must be more involved in situations in which he can watch others who are skilled at interacting with people.

An important part of modeling is *practice*. Once a child sees how others perform a certain skill, she can practice the skill herself. A child cannot learn to ride a bike simply by watching—she must eventually get on the bike and practice herself. This early practice will come with some help, of course. A parent may gently hold onto the bike or attach training wheels to help a child achieve balance. As the child becomes more self-confident and competent about riding, she can ride more independently. The same is true for social skills training—a child learning a new social skill will practice the behavior with some help in the beginning, but will do so more independently with time.

Another important part of modeling is *feedback*. Feedback refers to information given to a child about how a skill is performed. We all need feedback from skilled others when we learn something new. A child practicing bike riding can get some feedback from a parent about avoiding a large hill, pushing both feet on the pedal, and keeping her head up to see where she is going. The same process applies to your child's social skill training. As your child models and practices different social skills, feedback from you, teachers, and others will be important to correct flaws or help your child understand what needs minor adjustment. *Feedback should also include a lot of praise for your child's efforts and successes.*

Modeling, practice, and feedback are the cornerstones of learning social skills. Let's examine these processes more in the following sections to provide you with a good idea of how to develop better social skills in your child. Make sure your child is "on board" with these methods and ask him to start slowly. Encourage your child to put a lot of effort into the methods with the understanding that greater effort will lead to greater success.

Modeling

The best models for your child will be those closest to his age. Your child is not likely to care about what a much younger child does and may feel he cannot do what a much older child does. Many 10-year-old children look at what a 15-year-old child does and say "I can't do that." And sometimes they are right, they cannot, at least not yet. So let's include children near your child's age. These children could involve siblings, relatives, neighbors, classmates, or other peers. These children should be those your child knows fairly well so he is comfortable. *Make sure your models are socially skilled themselves (and not overly shy) and are willing and able to carry out tasks you ask them to do.*

Some parents say their child is so shy he will not speak to other children at all. You and your partner could be a good role model for social skills in this case. You can initially be the one who helps your child start and maintain a conversation. Keep in mind, however, that this strategy carries some risk. Some children are fine when speaking with their parents and their anxiety is low. Your child may be perfectly fine when speaking to you but then struggle with other children. Your child is welcome to practice his social skills with you but he will eventually need to practice with peers he does and does not know well.

If you have found some children near your child's age to act as models, then ask them to come over to your house (with their parents is fine). Let them know ahead of time what you will ask them to do—to practice some basic things such as talking to one another or asking someone for help. Ling's first task was to increase eye contact. If this is the case for your child, ask your models to have a brief conversation with each other as your shy child watches. The models can talk about whatever they want as long as they are polite and make good eye contact with each other.

Sit with your child to watch the brief conversation, which can be less than a minute. Ask your child to pay special attention to the specific skill on which you are working—in this case, eye contact. You may want to ask the models to repeat their conversation a few times so your child gets a good look at what is happening. If the models' parents give permission, you can videotape the conversation to show your child later how the children made good eye contact (see Box 5.1).

Practice and Feedback

If your child has a good feel for what he needs to do, then ask him to practice the skill with you and preferably with the models. In the case of eye contact, one of the models could speak to your child as your child simply holds his head up and makes good eye contact. Your child does not even have to speak—just listen and make eye contact. One of three things is likely to happen in this situation. Your child will make good eye contact throughout the brief interaction (again no longer than a minute), start to have good eye contact but then drift away during the conversation, or have great trouble making any eye contact with the model.

If your child made eye contact throughout the interaction, give him considerable praise for trying and for being successful! Even if your child made some eye contact during the conversation, give praise and show him what he did correctly. You can also encourage him to try a little harder next time and see if he can make eye contact the entire time. Try to get to a point at which he can make eye contact for at least a minute before going to the next step.

Box 5.1 Starting and maintaining conversations with others

The most important social skill your shy child should learn and practice is starting and maintaining conversations with others. Using modeling and other procedures from this chapter, spend a lot of time with your child about how to begin a conversation with others and how to keep the conversation going for at least a few minutes. Teach your shy child to:

- Ask questions about what the other kids are doing, such as the game being played.
- Ask to join a group activity.
- Discuss upcoming plans for the weekend or evening.
- Give compliments to other people.
- Invite someone to begin a new activity.
- Listen carefully to and acknowledge what others are saying.
- Share personal information such as a pet or recent movie seen.
- Talk about common interests such as what happened in class that day.
- Use manners to be polite and treat others with respect.
- Walk up to one or more people, smile, say "hello," and introduce himself.

Do not expect your child to have long conversations with others as you begin this teaching process. The main goal is to get him to talk more to others and see that doing so will lead to positive interactions and, hopefully, some friendships. Help your child understand that other people will not always be receptive to him and his social advances – some people are busy, mean, distracted, or just not interested at that time. Encourage your child to continue to seek people who do want to play and talk with him. It will happen!

If your child could not make any eye contact, praise him for trying. This is a skill that needs practice. Ask your child to make eye contact for just a few seconds and praise him for doing so. Gradually increase the amount of time he needs to maintain eye contact—perhaps from 2 to 4 to 6 to 8 seconds and so forth up to a minute. Do not be discouraged if your child cannot do this in 1 or 2 days. Your child may need to practice for several days or even a few weeks before he gets to the point at which he can maintain eye contact for a good amount of time.

Once your child can better maintain eye contact (or whatever skill is at the bottom of your list) with the models, have him practice this skill with family members and other people he commonly meets during the day. Remind your child to keep his head up and make eye contact when speaking. We want eye contact and other social skills to become something your child does almost automatically without thinking. Your child should also pay close attention to how others respond to him when he does make eye contact, such as talking to him more or paying greater attention to what he says. Increased eye contact and other social behaviors will hopefully lead to positive reactions from other people, such as smiles and invitations that serve as powerful rewards.

Other Social Skills

Modeling, practice, and feedback can eventually be applied to other skills on your child's list. Establishing eye contact for Ling was followed next by keeping her head up when speaking to others. Part of this skill was already in place once Ling could make better eye contact because she had to keep her head up to do so! Still, Ling needed to keep her head up when someone else was speaking to her. Again, use role models, ask your child to practice a skill, and provide feedback. This cycle must be continual.

As your child progresses up her list, she can develop and practice more complicated or more difficult social skills. Speaking in an audible tone of voice and accepting invitations from others to play were hard for Ling to do. She needed a lot of practice with her models and frequent feedback from her parents to speak up and be heard clearly. She was also encouraged to speak clearly when accepting invitations to play, such as saying "Yes, thank you, I would like to play." In doing so, she practiced other skills already developed, such as maintaining eye contact and keeping her head up.

Practicing in Public

You may find that your child does well in private situations such as at home but struggles more in public situations with other people. This is normal for shy children. As your child practices her social skills, however, she will need to practice more in public situations such as restaurants, shopping centers, and especially school. Accepting invitations to play is most crucial on the playground at school. Ling was eventually expected to respond to others in a positive way when they asked her to play. This included some cooperative work with school officials to set up these interactions and to encourage Ling to take advantage of them (see the later section regarding school officials).

Encourage your child to speak appropriately in public situations to help her practice important social skills. Combine the independent practices in Chapter 4 with the social skills training discussed here. At a restaurant, for example, ask your child to speak clearly and articulately and with good eye contact when ordering food. If this takes two or three practice attempts to get it right, that is okay! Again, give feedback to your child in a supportive way and praise her for effort and success. Another good strategy is to ask your child *after a situation* what he could have done differently. A shy child at a soccer game might say he could have done a better job of keeping his head up to talk to people or participate more in the game. Always challenge your child to practice and think about important social skills, especially in everyday situations.

Practicing social skills is important, but this is simply the *behavior* part of interacting with others. Some children must also learn about the *thinking* and *feeling* aspects of social behavior. *When we interact with others, we generally watch them closely to get an idea of what they may be thinking or feeling.* We look at body posture and facial expressions to help us decide what next to say and do. Shy children sometimes need help understanding how to "read" other people. In the next few sections, therefore, I focus on helping overly shy children take the perspective of others (thinking) and identify emotions in themselves and others (feeling).

Taking the Perspective of Others

An important social skill that many of us have is to understand and appreciate what another person is thinking and feeling. When we talk to a co-worker or partner, we watch how what we say affects the other person. Shy children often have difficulty appreciating what others say or feel because they are so wrapped up in themselves. They sometimes have trouble knowing how to respond to people who show different emotions in different situations.

Help your child take the perspective of others by using an *active observing and listening approach*. In this approach, a child is encouraged to occasionally stop what he is doing and look closely at other people to see what is happening. Recall that Ling walked around the playground with her head down, which meant she had little idea what other people were doing, thinking, or feeling. We might encourage Ling to occasionally stop walking, look carefully at other children on the playground, and note what they are doing. She may find that others are playing a game together, racing, or even arguing.

As children become better at observing others in natural situations, they can begin to comment more on what they see. You could encourage your overly shy child to list the names of children on the playground, write down what the children and teachers are doing, or tell you a story at dinnertime about what happened on the playground. You want your shy child to be an active observer of other people, which will draw her toward others and help her feel less alienated or alone.

As your child becomes an active observer of others, ask her to give you ideas about what people may be thinking and feeling in certain situations. As two children are racing, what might they be thinking? As two children are arguing, how might they be feeling? You can borrow a suggestion from Chapter 3 by noting everyday occurrences among people and asking your child to describe what she sees and what others may be thinking and doing.

The goal behind this process is to help your child become more aware of others and less afraid of what others think. Your child can realize that other children usually have the same kinds of thoughts and feelings she does—that other people are not different but are children just like her! A common mistake overly shy people make is believing that their personal worries and flaws are specific to them. They must realize that other people share the same worries and flaws. In doing so, you may find that your shy child needs more practice identifying emotions in others. I turn to this topic next.

Identifying Emotions

Another important part of social skills training is identifying emotions in yourself and others. Many overly shy children have trouble understanding why people say certain things to them and may withdraw as a result. Some children misinterpret the actions of other children as hostile or threatening when this is not true. A shy child may have someone accidentally bump into her in a crowded hallway and assume the person is angry with her. She may avoid that child and hallways in general. Another shy child might believe no one likes her because no one asks her to play, even though this might be because she declined several offers to play before.

I recommend teaching your overly shy child, especially a younger one, the difference between happy, sad, fearful/anxious, and angry emotions. A helpful way of doing this is to show your child pictures of people from magazines and ask him to identify which emotion is present. Shy children sometimes have trouble with this, so point out aspects of the picture such as smiles, frowns, facial tension, eye contact, body posture, and general context (such as two people arguing) to help pinpoint which emotion is present. Do not discuss very specific kinds of emotions such as jealousy or irritability or boredom—stick to basic ones such as happy, sad, fearful/anxious, and angry.

As your child becomes better at identifying emotions from pictures, try real-life scenes. Ask your child to examine different social interactions in his life at school and elsewhere to identify what emotions, if any, are present. Have him note how emotions can change from one person to another and from one situation to another. Ask your child if he can tell whether certain emotions are justified—should his friend Joe have gotten angry because someone went through his backpack (probably yes) or been happy when Jessica said her mom was sick (no).

Be sure your child can identify his own emotions as well. How does your child know he is happy, sad, fearful/anxious, or angry? Teach your child to rely on inner sensations such as muscle tension, burning ears, heart rate, and energy level to understand emotional differences. Ask your child what he is thinking during different emotional states. What thoughts does he have when he is happy about something? When he is angry with someone? When he is afraid? When he feels "blue"? Test this out in real-life scenes as well. When your child is obviously angry, ask him what emotion he feels and praise him for the right answer. Provide corrective feedback if he gives the wrong answer or does not know.

The long-term goal of this approach is to help a child better understand emotions and the perspective of others. An overly shy child may realize that not everyone is angry with her just because they do not play with her all the time. As children become better at identifying emotions, they can also see how their actions affect other people. Many shy children lower their head and avoid eye contact when others ask them to play. A shy child might realize that other people think she is angry with them based on her behavior. To change this, she could smile or show other signs of happiness to encourage contact with others. Combine modeling, practice, and feedback with an understanding of how others think and feel in social situations.

Social Skills and Independent Practice

In Chapter 4 I discussed different types of independent practices for overly shy children. As your child engages in these practices, he should perform various social skills and take the perspective of others and identify emotions. Let's discuss an example:

> Justin is a 14-year-old boy who has been working with his parents
> to increase his contact with peers and classmates. He has been
> overly shy for several years and rarely speaks to others at school or
> church. In recent months, Justin's parents have tried to get their
> son more involved with group activities, especially the teen group
> at church. They have worked with Justin to practice different
> situations that involve introducing himself to others and calling
> people on the telephone. More intense practices are forthcoming
> and include going on a group retreat with the church group and
> speaking before others in a class at school. Justin usually has
> problems speaking clearly to other people, however, so his parents
> wish to help their son with this behavior as well.

Justin is doing some admirable things such as introducing himself to others and calling people on the telephone. These are hard things for many teenagers to do, especially overly shy teenagers. Justin's practices are likely made more difficult, however, by poor social skills such as not speaking clearly. The sensible thing is to have Justin mix his practices with social skills training. How do we do that?

Before Justin engages in a certain practice (Chapter 4), his parents and others should help him practice the scene ahead of time. This is a *role play*. A role play is a scene acted out among people the teenager can trust to give him feedback and provide appropriate praise and guidance.

A teenager could role play calling someone on the telephone with a parent. *An important part of role play and practice is to have a clear goal in mind.* Justin should not simply call someone blindly to see what happens. There should be a purpose to the call—perhaps asking about a homework assignment, checking on the status of a sick or absent classmate, or asking someone to the movies this weekend.

Once this goal is established, set a timeline for the role play. This timeline can first be short (2 minutes) and then gradually longer (5–10 minutes). The next step is to practice with your child in the form of a role play. You could play the role of the person being called and your child could be himself. The role play should be as real as possible, so have your child call you on the telephone from another area of the house. During the first role play, give immediate feedback to your child about his social skills. For example, is he loud enough on the telephone to be heard and articulate enough to be understood? The following is an example:

(Telephone rings)

You:	Hello.
Your child:	Hi ... this ... is Justin.
You:	Hi Justin, how are you?
Your child:	(long pause) Ah ... well ... I'm good I guess.
You:	(stepping out of the role play for some feedback) Okay Justin, speak up a little more because it's hard to hear you. Thanks.
Your child:	Okay (louder this time) Hi, this is Justin.
You:	Hi Justin, how are you?
Your child:	Good I guess (long pause again).
You:	Thanks for calling. Is there something you needed?
Your child:	Ah, yeah, I guess, I was calling about the homework.
You:	(stepping out of the role play for some feedback) Okay, Justin, that's good, try to be a little more specific about why you are calling.
Your child:	Okay. I was calling to see if you know the homework assignment from math class today. He put it up on the board like a minute before class ended and I couldn't get all of it down.
You:	Great job! (stepping back into the role play). Yes, hang on, let me get that for you. It's page 77, problems 1–9 and 12–19.

Your child: Great, thanks so much for the help.
          You: You are welcome, thanks for calling.
Your child: Goodbye.
          You: Goodbye.

After this role play, discuss with your child the positive social behaviors he showed, especially effort and responding to feedback. Point out areas that can be worked on as well, such as speaking up, talking more clearly, and avoiding long pauses in the conversation. Practicing good manners, such as saying "thank you" for the homework assignment, is a good idea as well. Practice this role play a few more times with immediate feedback until your child does well. The next step is then to practice the role play with no immediate feedback. The feedback during these later role plays will come *after* the conversation or other task.

Once your child practices a task with good social skills a number of times, then he can try the scene on his own. Remind your child that the actual scene may be different than the role play. The child at the other end of the telephone will obviously not say the identical things you said during the role play. You are welcome to watch or listen to your child as he calls, and certainly you should give your child feedback afterward. Praise his effort because doing these things is very hard for an overly shy child.

Other kinds of scenes can also involve social skills practice (see Table 5.1 for suggestions regarding specific social skills). Justin will be expected to introduce himself to other people. This is something he and his parents or others can practice before doing so in real life situations. As Justin engages in even more intense scenes, such as attending group retreats and giving oral presentations at school, he will need to practice various social skills. These scenes can be practiced first in a safe situation. Justin could give a presentation before family members or maintain a conversation with peers from his church group.

Your child should practice her social skills each day. This is best done with actual peers and friends but can also be part of a family activity on a quiet day. Do not assume your child is fine once she can tackle a few role plays. Instead, adopt the attitude that social skills training and practice in social and performance situations are lifelong processes. Your child will do much better with practice in a short period of time, but extended practice is needed to truly master anxiety and social skills.

Table 5.1 Suggestions regarding important social skills in children and adolescents

Accepting invitations from others for play or other social interaction

→ Maintain eye contact and smile, ask what others are doing, say "thank you" and begin to play

Accepting praise and compliments from others

→ Maintain eye contact and smile, say "thank you," perhaps offer a compliment to the other person in return

Answering the door or telephone

→ Clearly say "hello" or "how can I help you?," maintain good distance, take message

Asking others for help or information

→ Know exactly what information is needed, ask appropriately ("Excuse me"), be clear in asking for help

Being assertive in saying "no" or when asking for something

→ Make eye contact, be brief in saying no, state your intention clearly and with good voice volume

Calling someone on the telephone or inviting someone for a fun activity

→ Speak clearly and articulately, know ahead of time what the topic is, use manners

Controlling impulses and anger instead of acting quickly upon them

→ Count silently to ten, relax body, exit situation appropriately, talk to someone

Cooperating with others in a game or project

→ Use manners, take turns, engage in small conversation, thank others for playing

Dealing with being sad or anxious

→ Relax body, think about difficult thoughts, understand the feeling is temporary, talk to someone

Dealing with embarrassing or stressful situations such as teasing

→ Ignore provocation, walk away, go to a safe area, talk to someone if teasing is severe

Delaying gratification, such as completing schoolwork before playing or television

→ Schedule a time to do homework, focus on future reward of doing work first, praise self for waiting

Eating appropriately around others

→ Chew food slowly, speak when mouth is empty of food, relax body, listen to others

Giving affection

→ Know the right situation to give affection, know what kinds of affection are acceptable and to whom, keep affection small in scope, mix affection with compliments

Greeting others appropriately

→ Say "hello" and smile, keep head up, speak articulately and with good voice volume

Identifying emotions in oneself and others, such as happiness, sadness, fear/anxiety, and anger

→ Watch body posture and facial expressions, listen to statements made by a person, study the context of the situation (what is happening around the people involved)

Initiating and maintaining conversations with others

→ Think about what topic to focus on, make eye contact, speak clearly, ask questions

Introducing oneself or other people

→ Use appropriate greeting, pick a good time, use full sentence, follow-up with questions

Joining activities with peers

→ Introduce self, ask others if they want another person to join, speak clearly and with confidence

Keeping head up when speaking to others

→ Maintain eye contact with person, smile, maintain conversation, ask questions

Listening to others appropriately

→ Nod head occasionally, maintain eye contact, smile, do not interrupt

Continued

Table 5.1 cont'd

Maintaining eye contact with others during a conversation

→ Keep head up, watch the facial expression of the person talking, smile

Maintaining personal hygiene and grooming

→ Wash and brush teeth appropriately, dress nicely, use deodorant, comb hair, fix clothes

Ordering a meal in a food establishment

→ Keep head up, maintain eye contact, speak articulately and with good voice volume, listen attentively to the person taking the order

Performing athletically before others

→ Stay involved with group activity, try doing your best, talk to others, have fun

Refraining from interrupting or inappropriately touching other people

→ Maintain eye contact, wait for other person to stop talking, maintain appropriate distance (2-3 feet) from person talking

Refraining from rude behaviors such as yelling, insults, sarcasm, or hitting

→ Watch own behavior closely, use manners, listen carefully, control anger

Resisting group pressure to do something inappropriate

→ Think whether someone is asking you to do something inappropriate, say "no" clearly, give reason for saying no, walk away from the situation, avoid tempting situations

Resolving conflicts with others

→ Negotiate solutions to problems without force, listen carefully to others' opinions, think about all sides of the problem, develop a solution agreeable to everyone

Sharing feelings appropriately

→ Discuss feelings when not angry, use manners, speak articulately and listen carefully to others' reactions

Speaking articulately

→ Speak slowly and pronounce each syllable clearly, maintain eye contact, watch others' reactions, speak with good voice volume

Speaking in a clear and audible tone of voice

→ Speak slowly, listen to self to see if voice volume is strong, maintain eye contact, watch others' reactions

Speaking or reading before others

→ Speak slowly and articulately, speak with good voice volume, relax body, practice beforehand, be well prepared

Taking the perspective of other people

→ Actively observe and listen to others, think about what others may be thinking and feeling in a certain situation, ask others what they were thinking and feeling

Taking turns when playing a game

→ Wait patiently, smile, thank others for playing and for your turn, be gracious in winning or losing

Using manners

→ Make eye contact, use "please," "thank you," and "excuse me" appropriately in complete sentences, watch others' reactions

Writing before others

→ Relax body and fingers, write slowly and carefully, focus on task at hand

Continue to work closely as well with adults who supervise your child, such as school officials.

Working with School Officials in Social Skills Training

Shy children generally have most difficulty in school-related social and performance situations (Chapter 4). These situations cause the most distress and lead to greatest avoidance so they must receive a great deal of attention. Working with school officials with respect to social skills training is important for this reason and because they are with your child for several hours per day. School officials are in a unique position to help your child practice social skills and give feedback. Meet with key school officials such as your child's guidance counselor to set up a plan whereby your child can practice important social skills during his school-based practices. Include teachers who supervise social and performance behaviors, especially those from physical education, English, choir, and band.

Share with school officials your plan for getting your child more involved in group activities and practicing social skills and exposures. School officials will likely inform you what they can and cannot do, so be patient but assertive. Some school districts may allow you to establish a 504 plan that allows for special accommodations for children with a condition that interferes with learning, so ask about this as well. Most importantly, set up specific opportunities that school officials can implement to help your child become more social and perform well before others. Share your hopes about what kind of feedback you want your child to receive and offer to help.

As your child practices social skills in more school-based situations, follow up with school officials about his progress. Daily emails, conversations, or report cards are useful (Chapter 2). As you receive feedback from school officials, pass the information on to your child and talk about what was done well and what needs more work. Speak to school officials about obstacles or threats that face your child and that prevent her from appropriate social interactions and performances before others. Be sure as well to show your appreciation to school officials who are most helpful during this process.

Do's and Don'ts

Here are a few reminders of do's and don'ts on your part:

Do

- Identify social skills that are most difficult for your child.
- Find models of good social behavior for your child.
- Have your child practice social skills with models.
- Give feedback to your child about his effort and effectiveness at social skills.
- Have your child practice social skills in public situations and independent practices.
- Help your child take the perspective of others.
- Help your child identify correct emotions in himself and others.
- Work closely with school officials to develop your child's social skills.

Don't

- Rescue your child from all social situations.
- Ask your child to practice interacting with others without proper social skills.
- Avoid bringing others in to help, such as peer models or teachers.

What Is Next?

Social skills are an important part of interacting with others. Shy children often have fewer opportunities to practice good social skills. Attempts to help shy children become more social and perform well before others must therefore include much practice and feedback about these skills. Your child will look to you for guidance about how to address others, so be patient and persistent when teaching him important social skills. Being patient and persistent will bear fruit when you see your child interact more with others and see the positive things that happen when he does so. There are other things you and your child can do to ease the stress of social and performance situations, and these are discussed in Chapter 6.

6

Helping a Child Relax and Think More Realistically

Ryan is an 8-year-old boy who is very shy and quiet in his classroom. He rarely speaks to others and seems quite nervous when asked to speak. Ryan says he sometimes has stomachaches in class and feels "shaky." His teacher says that Ryan sometimes "gets all worked up" when asked to read in class or participate in some group activity. She said Ryan will either "breathe fast" or appears so rigid that he does not seem to be breathing regularly. Ryan's teacher often tells him to calm down or sit at his seat with his head down to try to relax. Ryan has visited the school nurse three times this year after complaining of not feeling well, though his parents say their son seems fine at home.

Amanda is a 15-year-old girl who is new to high school and seems overwhelmed by the whole scene. She has always been a shy person but she seems even more socially isolated this year. Her parents and guidance counselor have worked with Amanda to get her more involved in two extracurricular activities and one team sport, which Amanda has been willing to do. Amanda reports, however, that she feels very tense in these situations and wishes she could be more physically comfortable around others.

This chapter will cover the following topics:

- Helping your child feel more comfortable in social situations by practicing proper breathing.
- Helping your child feel more comfortable in social situations by practicing muscle relaxation.
- Helping your child feel more comfortable in social situations by managing worrisome thoughts that could lead to avoidance.

Children such as Ryan and Amanda often have physical symptoms of nervousness when interacting with others or performing before others. These symptoms, which were discussed in Chapters 1 and 2, commonly include headaches, stomachaches, breathlessness, hyperventilation, blushing, trembling, increased heart rate, muscle tension, or sweating. If your child has any of these or other physical symptoms, then I recommend a *full examination by a physician* to rule out possible medical problems. Many overly shy children have physical symptoms of nervousness *only* when interacting with others, especially people they do not know well. This indicates that the physical symptoms are due to nervousness and not a medical problem, but it is always better to be safe and have your child checked for medical conditions.

If your overly shy child has physical symptoms of distress but no medical condition, then some of the methods in this chapter may be useful to help him relax. These methods include two exercises to reduce physical symptoms of distress when your child practices interacting with others. The methods are most helpful when used with the independent practice methods in Chapter 4. If your child is ready to start a conversation with a classmate, for example, she may find it helpful to use the methods presented next to manage physical symptoms of tension and feel more relaxed during her interaction.

Physical symptoms of nervousness sometimes lead to worrisome thoughts and thus avoidance of social and performance situations (Chapter 2). I discuss ways to help your child manage worrisome thoughts later in this chapter. Helping a child manage physical symptoms may help him worry less and be more relaxed and confident when interacting with others. Amanda, for example, may find she can more easily approach and "fit in" with a group of people if she feels more confident that she will not be so tense and physically uncomfortable.

Different methods to help a child control physical feelings of distress are available, but I concentrate here on methods that are most *feasible, portable,* and *time-efficient.* In other words, these methods can be practiced easily by most children, can be used in most settings, and take only a short time to do. Two methods in particular involve managing breathing and using progressive muscle relaxation. These methods are discussed separately, but both can be used to reduce physical feelings of distress.

Breathing

A simple way to help your child reduce physical feelings of distress is to teach him to breathe correctly. Many children experience shortness of breath, breathe shallowly, or hyperventilate when upset. Doing so actually makes the feeling of anxiety worse, so helping a child regulate his breathing is important. Ask your child to sit in a comfortable position. *Then ask him to breathe in slowly through his nose (with his mouth closed) and breathe out slowly through his mouth.* As your child does so, encourage him to breathe deeply into his diaphragm (between the abdomen and chest and just below the rib cage). Your child may need to push two fingers into his diaphragm to experience the sensation of a full, deep breath. He can then breathe slowly out of his mouth. You may even join the process to help your child practice at home.

For younger children such as Ryan, create an image during the breathing method. Ryan could imagine blowing up a tire or pretend he is a large, floating balloon. As Ryan breathes in, he can imagine filling up with fuel and energy. As he breathes out, he can imagine losing fuel or energy (or tension). Your child must come to understand the difference between feeling tense when his lungs are full of air and feeling more relaxed after breathing out. The following breathing script may be helpful (adapted from Kearney & Albano, 2007):

> Pretend you are a hot air balloon. When you breathe in, you are filling the balloon with air so it can go anywhere you want. Breathe in through your nose like this (show for your child). Breathe slowly and deeply—try to breathe in a lot of air! Now breathe out slowly through your mouth like air leaving a balloon. Count slowly in your head as you breathe out ... 1 ... 2 ... 3 ... 4 ... 5. Let's try this again (practice at least three times).

Your child should use this breathing method in situations in which he feels most tense and especially during situations on his hierarchy (Chapter 4). The breathing method is nice because a child can practice this method without drawing much attention from others. Have your child practice this breathing method at least three times a day for a few minutes at a time. In addition, ask your child to practice in the morning before school and during particularly stressful times at school. Some children benefit as well by practicing this method whenever they are around other people and may have to speak to them. Ryan, for example, could practice breathing correctly right before he reads to his class or Amanda could practice breathing correctly right before she joins a team meeting. In what situations do you think your child could best practice this method?

Muscle Relaxation

Another way to help a child reduce physical feelings of distress is progressive muscle relaxation. Youths such as Ryan or Amanda are usually quite tense in different areas of their body, especially in the shoulders, face, and stomach. Different methods of muscle relaxation are available, but a preferred one is a *tension-release method* in which a child physically tenses, holds, and then releases a specific muscle group. For example, a child may ball his hand into a fist, squeeze as tightly as possible and hold the tension for 10 seconds, and then suddenly release the grip (try it). When this is done two or three times in a row, people generally report feelings of warmth in the muscle as well as relaxation. The idea is to replace anxious feelings with more relaxed ones so your child may feel more comfortable speaking to others or performing before others.

Muscle relaxation via tension-release can be done in different ways. When I work with children, I use a relaxation script that covers most areas of the body. I first ask the child to sit in a comfortable position and close her eyes. I then read the script slowly and ask the child to participate. You may wish to use the following script with your child (adapted from Ollendick & Cerny, 1981).

(Speaking slowly and in a low voice) Okay, sit down, try to relax, and close your eyes. Try to make your body droopy and floppy, as if you are a wet towel. Take your right hand and squeeze it as hard as you can. Hold it tight! (Wait 5–10 seconds.) Now let go quickly. Good job. Let's do that again. Take your right hand and squeeze it as hard as you can. Hold it. (Wait 5–10 seconds.) Now let go quickly. See how that feels. Nice and warm and loose. Now take your left hand and squeeze it as hard as you can. Hold it tight! (Wait 5–10 seconds.) Now let go quickly. Good job. Let's do that again. Take your left hand and squeeze it as hard as you can. Hold it. (Wait 5–10 seconds.) Now let go quickly. See how that feels. Nice and warm and loose.

Now shrug your shoulders hard and push them up to your ears. Make your shoulders really tight. Hold them there. (Wait 5–10 seconds.) Now let go quickly. Great. Let's do that again. Shrug your shoulders hard and push them up to your ears. Make your shoulders really tight. Hold them there. (Wait 5–10 seconds.) Now let go quickly. Great job.

Now scrunch up your face as much as you can. Make your face seem really small and tight. Now hold it there. (Wait 5–10 seconds.) Now let your face go droopy. Good. Let's do that again. Scrunch up your face as much as you can. Make your face seem really small and tight. Now hold it there. (Wait 5–10 seconds.) Now let your face go droopy. Good job.

Now I want you to bite down real hard with your teeth. Make your jaw really tight. Hold it there. (Wait 5–10 seconds.) Now open your jaw. How does that feel? Good. Let's try that again. Bite down real hard with your teeth. Make your jaw really tight. Hold it there. (Wait 5–10 seconds.) Now open your jaw. Try to make it as loose as you can. Good practicing!

Let's go to your stomach now. Bring in your stomach as much as you can—make it real tight! Press it against your backbone. Now hold it there. (Wait 5–10 seconds.) Now let go quickly. That feels better. Let's try that again. Bring in your stomach as much as you can – make it real tight! Press it against your backbone. Now hold it there. (Wait 5–10 seconds.) Now let go quickly. Great job.

Okay, one more. Push your feet onto the floor real hard so your legs feel really tight. Push hard! Now hold it. (Wait 5–10 seconds.) Now relax your legs. Shake them a little. Let's try that again. Push your feet onto the floor real hard so your legs feel really tight. Push hard! Now hold it. (Wait 5–10 seconds.) Now relax your legs. Shake them a little. Good practicing!

Now try to make your whole body really droopy—pretend you are a wet towel! Relax your whole body and see how nice that feels. You did a great job relaxing. Okay, open your eyes.

Ask your child to practice this script at least twice per day, perhaps in the morning before school and at night before bed. You could also encourage her to use commercially available breathing and relaxation tapes if she finds those more helpful. You may wish to teach your child these breathing and muscle relaxation methods at one time so she can use one or both right away. Some children prefer one approach over the other, which is fine. Your child should practice and use the methods as soon as possible, however.

Your time and your child's time may be limited, especially during school situations that can be quite hectic. In this case, you may wish to help your child use breathing and *partial* muscle relaxation. In partial muscle relaxation, you or your child chooses one or two areas of his body that are particularly tense and your child practices the tension-release method *only on those areas*. Ryan, for example, may say his shoulders and stomach are tensest when asked to speak. To save time, he could concentrate his relaxation efforts on these two areas.

Proper breathing and muscle relaxation are *most* important to use when your child practices the social and performance situations on his hierarchy (Chapter 4). In fact, you may wish to teach your child these breathing and relaxation methods immediately after developing a hierarchy. In addition, encourage your child to practice these breathing and relaxation methods during times you know he is particularly distressed at school. You may need to solicit the help of a guidance counselor or teachers who can take your child aside and help her practice relaxing. Some children benefit from practicing these methods in a counselor's office immediately before a stressful situation.

Addressing Worrisome Thoughts

Another part of shyness for some children is worrisome thoughts they have in social and performance situations. These thoughts sometimes begin following physical symptoms or they can lead to physical symptoms and avoidance of different situations. Consider the following case:

> Neda is a 14-year-old girl who has always been shy and quiet but seems more so in high school. She is withdrawn at school and says she worries a lot about being embarrassed, blushing before others, having to talk to boys, and performing athletically during physical education class. Neda says she does not like to eat in the school cafeteria because of the noise there and worries that people will ridicule the way she eats. She also has many doubts about herself and blames herself for many things. Neda's worries have led to considerable muscle tension and stomachaches and she has asked her parents to explore nontraditional methods of schooling for her.

Overly shy adolescents such as Neda often worry about bad things happening in social and performance situations. Neda worries about being embarrassed or being ridiculed by others, which causes her to feel physically uneasy and leads her to think about ways to avoid anxious situations. Some nervousness about social and performance situations is normal because many people get uptight when meeting people for the first time or when speaking before others. Most people are able to "set aside" their worries and go about doing what they need to do. For overly shy children such as Neda, however, worry can be so strong that it causes considerable distress and prevents them from doing what they would like to do.

I mentioned in Chapter 2 that children such as Neda sometimes worry that terrible things will happen in social situations (especially embarrassment or humiliation) or think wrongly about how other people are judging them. They also tend to do the following:

- Assume that external events are their fault when this is not the case.
- Assume that one bad event means all such events will be negative.
- Believe that events are either good or bad, with no middle ground.
- Believe that social interactions are dangerous or threatening.
- Believe the world "should" operate a certain way.
- Believe they will always be excluded or ignored by others.
- Believe they will appear foolish, nervous, incompetent, or inadequate before others.
- Dismiss positive events, such as a compliment, as negative or trivial.
- Evaluate a situation as much worse than it really is.
- Focus much more on the negative than the positive in a social situation.
- Make a conclusion about a social situation that is neither realistic nor based on evidence.
- Predict future terrible events such as ridicule even without supporting evidence.
- Remember negative aspects of a situation and forget positive ones.

Neda had several of these beliefs. She felt she would be ridiculed in physical education class and in the school cafeteria and believed these and other situations were much worse than they really were. She also had doubts about her abilities in social and performance situations and focused much more on the negative than the positive in these situations. Neda assumed bad things would happen in social and performance situations even though not much evidence supported her beliefs. Neda's inaccurate, worrisome thoughts then led to physical distress and a desire to avoid or escape different situations.

Worrisome thoughts are generally truer of adolescents than children. Adolescents aged 11–17 years usually have better thinking skills than children aged 10 years or younger, so they tend to worry more. Younger children tend to have briefer thoughts such as "I don't want to go" and cannot say why they do not want to attend a certain social activity. The methods described next are thus generally more suited to adolescents than children. If you feel your younger child might benefit from some of these methods, however, feel free to try them. Otherwise, you may wish to concentrate on the other methods in this book, such as practice (Chapters 3 and 4), social skills training (Chapter 5), and relaxation and breathing training (earlier in this chapter).

Managing Worrisome Thoughts

What can we do to help children such as Neda and your overly shy child? Keep in mind that the main goal here is to help your child think more *realistically* in social and performance situations. Notice that I did *not* say "think more positively." Telling your child to "think happy thoughts," to "not worry," to "try not to think about it," or that she is a "wonderful child" will not work! If your child worries about bad things happening in social and performance situations, that is okay. But your child *must also think more realistically* about what is actually happening in these situations.

Neda worries that "everyone will stare at me and laugh at me during physical education class." We cannot change the fact that certain thoughts pop into Neda's head—thoughts and worries are normal things that occur unexpectedly. Therefore, we would *not* want to tell Neda "Stop thinking those thoughts" or "Don't worry" because, when these thoughts *do* pop into her head—and they will—she will become even more distressed ("They told me not to worry but I can't help it!"). If someone told you *not* to think about blue dogs for the next minute, for example, what happens? You think about blue dogs!

Having a worrisome thought is fine *as long as* your overly shy child takes a step back, thinks about the thought, and develops a more realistic thought. Neda could think during physical education class that everyone is staring at her and then become anxious. Her anxiety will continue if she does not pause, think about what she is thinking, and think more realistically about what is happening. She could, for example, look around, see that other people are running about or talking to one another or even looking at her. Neda could then develop a more realistic thought such as "Some people might be looking at me, but not everyone is." Her anxiety in class should then decrease a little.

Notice that Neda did not try to block her original worrisome thought. I tell teenagers that it is okay to have a worrisome thought but to *just let the thought pass through your body*. Even if a teenager has multiple worries or has the same thought over and over, I tell her that thoughts are not dangerous and that thoughts are like phantoms or specters that have no real weight or worth. They are not harmful and they can just pass through the body. This image and task often help an adolescent reduce the burden or power of the worrisome thought.

Notice also that Neda did not develop a "happy" thought in reaction to her worrisome thought. She did not think "Everything is wonderful" or "I am great" or "I should not be worrying." *Instead, she developed a more realistic thought based on the evidence.* She looked around and saw that a few people were looking in her direction *but not everyone*. When we think more realistically, we understand that the horrible things we imagine are not actually happening and we often feel less distressed.

If you decide you want to work with your child to help her develop more realistic thoughts, keep several important things in mind:

- You and your child should have a good relationship with good communication.
- Your child should be fairly verbal and be willing to discuss her worries in detail. I recommend the methods in the following section for children at least age 11 years. However, you may have a precocious younger child who could benefit from these methods.
- Your child should have fairly good social skills (Chapter 5).
- Your child must be motivated to change her worrisome thoughts and practice the methods discussed here in different social and performance situations.
- The methods discussed next will not work if your child faces legitimate threats from others. If everyone were truly staring at Neda and laughing at her during physical education class, then her thoughts would indeed be realistic and we would not want to change them. In this situation, the legitimate threat from others would have to be addressed first.

The next sections cover types of worrisome thoughts that overly shy children often have in social and performance situations as well as specific methods to help your child with these thoughts. If you find that your child's worries are so strong that they cannot be changed or managed, then I recommend consulting a qualified mental health professional (Chapter 1).

Identifying Worrisome Thoughts

What kinds of worrisome thoughts do older children and adolescents have in social and performance situations? I mentioned several brief ones earlier, but in my experience overly shy children tend to worry or make the following mistakes in their thinking:

- They assume that something bad *is happening* when actually it is not. Neda assumed others were laughing at her in physical education class when actually others were mostly involved in their own activities.
- They assume terrible things *will happen* when terrible things are not likely to happen. For example, a teenager may assume that other children will push or shove him in the hallway at school even though the chances of this actually happening are quite small.
- They assume other people are thinking about them even though they cannot know. This is called "mindreading." For example, a teenager may assume others believe she is repulsive when she has no real knowledge of this.
- They jump to conclusions from just one event or make "mountains out of molehills" by assuming that the consequences of their acts will be extremely terrible. For example, a teenager may worry that speaking to someone new will result in immediate social rejection by most people in the school.
- They assume they will be embarrassed and that the embarrassment will be horrible. For example, a teenager may assume she will look foolish in some way, become embarrassed, and feel so mortified that she can never attend school again.
- They see situations only as either perfect or terrible and not somewhere in between. For example, a teenager may assume that a conversation with an acquaintance was very awkward even though some aspects of the conversation were positive.

- They focus much more on the negative than the positive side of things. For example, a teenager who performed at a recital may concentrate a lot on some wrong notes played instead of the good overall performance of the musical piece.
- They blame themselves for things that are not within their control. For example, a teenager may become upset that a group project went poorly and blame herself instead of the group.

Do any of these sound familiar to you or your child? Are there other examples of worrisome thoughts your child has in social or performance situations that make her very upset? Use Worksheet 6.1: *in the first column,* ask your child to list all social or performance situations that cause her great distress. These situations will likely mirror those discussed in Chapters 3 and 4, but others could apply. *In the second column,* ask your child to list her worrisome thoughts in these situations. Update these lists once a week as you work with your child. Photocopy this worksheet as much as you need.

Methods to Manage Worrisome Thoughts

Now that you have identified and charted your child's worrisome thoughts in social and performance situations, begin to work to challenge and change them. I recommend having a discussion with your child each evening about any worrisome thoughts he had that day in a social or performance situation. Adolescents sometimes have difficulty with this process, which is okay. Do not badger your child to produce thoughts. Concentrate instead on worrisome thoughts that seem particularly strong or distressful that day. If your child says he did not have

Worksheet 6.1

Social/performance situations that bother me ("S")   My thoughts in this situation ("T")

Other, more realistic thoughts ("O")   Praise myself ("P")

any worries or that his thoughts were not distressful, then leave him be. Some youths have distressing thoughts only once in a while. If he did have a particularly upsetting thought or worry that day, then the methods in this section may be helpful.

As you discuss your child's worrisome thoughts with him, encourage him to think about the acronym **STOP** (adapted from Silverman & Kurtines, 1996):

- **S:** Am I **S**cared or nervous about a certain social or performance situation?
- **T:** What **T**houghts am I having in this situation?
- **O:** What **O**ther, more realistic thoughts can I have?
- **P:** **P**raise myself for thinking more realistic thoughts

Your child first needs to identify social and performance situations that cause her the most distress. These situations were likely identified in Chapters 3 and 4 and can be listed under Column 1 in Worksheet 6.1. New social and performance situations that give your child difficulty can be added to Column 1 as needed. When in a new social or performance situation, your child should ask herself "Am I currently *Scared* or nervous?" If the answer to this question is "yes," then that situation should be added to Column 1.

As you have your daily discussion with your child, review his list of social and performance situations (S), see if they occurred that day, and see whether your child had a worrisome thought in each situation. As you and your child discuss these thoughts, *do not be judgmental or critical.* Having negative thoughts is a normal human experience—we simply have to be sure that worrisome thoughts are balanced and eventually replaced with more realistic thoughts.

If your child did have a particularly worrisome thought that day, then label this thought as the "T" part of STOP. This thought would be listed in Column 2 of Worksheet 6.1. Recall that Neda's thought in physical education class was that "everyone will stare at me and laugh at me during physical education class." Physical education class would thus be listed in Column 1 and her worrisome thought would be listed in Column 2.

Your child must identify which situations cause her the most distress and then "think about her own thoughts" in these situations so she can work to manage them. If your child can get into the practice of writing down her worrisome thoughts *during* a social or performance situation, then this is even more helpful. Ask your child to keep a written log of her thoughts in these situations so that you and she can discuss them later. Whenever your child is in a social or performance situation that causes her distress, she should practice the "S" and "T" portions of STOP as much as possible.

If your child listed a worrisome thought (T) in a social or performance situation, then she should think about *other, more realistic thoughts*—this is the "O" part of STOP. I discuss these other thoughts in the next section. Finally, if your child was able to think more realistic thoughts in this situation, then she should silently *praise herself* for doing so—this is the "P" part of STOP. Your child can say things such as "Good job!," "Great thinking!," or "I am proud of myself."

Ask your child to practice the STOP method as much as possible when she is distressed in a social or performance situation. Your child should practice this method so it becomes automatic or "secondhand." In other words, your child should practice developing more realistic thoughts in a given situation and come to realize that the chances of bad things happening are actually low and that the consequences of most situations are not that bad. Let's talk next about developing more realistic thoughts—the "O" part of STOP.

More Realistic Thoughts

Once your child can easily complete the "S" and "T" portions of STOP, then you and she can move to the next step. As you and your child discuss her worrisome thoughts, ask her to keep the following questions in mind as she challenges these thoughts (adapted from Kearney & Albano, 2007):

> *Am I 100% sure this will happen (or is happening)?*
> *Can I really know what that person thinks of me?*
> *What's the worst thing that can really happen?*
> *Have I ever been in this situation before, and was it really that bad?*
> *How many times has this terrible thing actually happened?*
> *Am I the only person who has ever had to deal with this situation?*
> *So what if I'm not perfect in this situation?*
> *Is this really my fault?*

Let's discuss some examples of worrisome thoughts that overly shy children have in social and performance situations and illustrate some conversations you could have with your child to help him develop more realistic thoughts. We'll do so with an eye on the questions listed here. The point of this exercise is to take a step back after a worrisome thought and analyze it carefully based on the evidence at hand. These conversations were introduced for youths with school refusal behavior but apply to overly shy children as well (Kearney, 2007).

One type of negative thought occurs when a teenager assumes terrible things are happening when in fact they are not. For example, a teenager might assume others are laughing at her when entering a classroom when actually others are laughing at a joke. If your child has this kind of thought, encourage her to develop more realistic thoughts by thinking about what other explanations are more likely. Use Worksheet 6.1, the STOP method, and questions outlined above:

> *You:* Okay, you wrote down that your "S" today was when you walked into class and that you thought ("T") other kids might be laughing at you when you went into class, right?
>
> *Your child:* Yeah, they were all joking around and I felt really bad.
>
> *You:* Okay, so let's talk about the "O" part, some other thoughts you could have—are you 100% sure that they were laughing at you? Be honest.
>
> *Your child:* Not 100% I guess, I don't know.
>
> *You:* Okay, good. What else might have been going on?
>
> *Your child:* I don't know.
>
> *You:* Well, let's think about it. What else could they have been laughing at?
>
> *Your child:* They're always joking around, saying dumb things. I guess they could have been doing that.
>
> *You:* Great job coming up with a different thought! Yeah, you're right, maybe they were laughing at something else because that's what they do?
>
> *Your child:* Yeah, I guess that could have been happening [then praise ("P") this new thought].

Another type of negative thought many teenagers have is assuming terrible things are going to happen. For example, a teenager who has to talk to other kids at school may assume that others will not speak to her. If your child has this kind of thought, encourage her to develop more realistic thoughts by thinking about the worst thing that can actually happen and how many times this terrible thing has actually happened.

Use Worksheet 6.1, the STOP method, and questions outlined above:

> *You*: Okay, you wrote down that your "S" today was being nervous about talking to those kids about your homework assignment and that you thought ("T") they would ignore you, right?
>
> *Your child*: Yeah, I figured they would just look away.
>
> *You*: Okay, so let's talk about the "O" part. What was the worst thing that could have happened if they ignored you? What would happen then? Be honest.
>
> *Your child*: Well, I'd look like an idiot I guess.
>
> *You*: Okay, good. Even if the worst thing happened, and you felt kind of dumb, what could you do then?
>
> *Your child*: I'd just ask somebody else.
>
> *You*: Great! So, even if the worst thing happened, you could handle it, right?
>
> *Your child*: Yeah, that's true.
>
> *You*: And how many times have the other kids just completely ignored you?
>
> *Your child*: Well, it did happen once, but usually people are nice.
>
> *You*: So…
>
> *Your child*: So I guess that the other kids won't usually ignore me, but if they do, I can just ask somebody else.
>
> *You*: Great job! ("P").

Another type of negative thought many teenagers have is assuming they know what other people are thinking—this is called "mindreading." Teenagers who are nervous in social and performance situations sometimes think they know what others are thinking and that those thoughts must be bad. For example, teenagers playing a musical instrument may assume that audience members think their performance is terrible, and so they become distressed. If your child has this kind of thought, encourage her to develop more realistic thoughts by thinking about what other explanations are more likely and whether she really knows what others are thinking. Use Worksheet 6.1, the STOP method, and questions outlined above:

> *You*: Okay, you wrote down that your "S" today was the recital and that you thought ("T") the audience thought your performance was awful, right?

Your child: Yeah, I made some mistakes and I'm sure they thought I couldn't play.

You: Okay, so let's talk about the "O" part. Are you 100% sure that they were thinking that? Can you really know what other people are thinking about you? Be honest.

Your child: No, I was so busy reading the music I couldn't really look at the audience.

You: Okay, good. What else might they have been thinking?

Your child: I don't know, maybe that I made some mistakes?

You: Well, maybe, but you were playing in a full orchestra, right? When someone makes a mistake, can the audience really tell?

Your child: Not really. You can only tell the music is off when everybody is making a whole bunch of mistakes. Maybe they couldn't tell about me.

You: Great job coming up with a different thought! ("P") Yeah, you're right, maybe they didn't notice your mistakes because you're just one player in the orchestra?

Your child: Yeah, I guess that's right.

Another type of negative thought occurs when teenagers jump to conclusions from just one event or make "mountains out of molehills." They may assume the consequences of their actions will be extremely terrible. For example, a teenager could assume that she is going to fail a course based on one bad test score. If your child has this kind of thought, encourage her to develop more realistic thoughts by thinking about what other explanations are more likely and whether the consequence (failing) is really likely to happen. Use Worksheet 6.1, the STOP method, and questions outlined above:

You: Okay, you wrote down that your "S" today was that you got a poor grade on your test and that you thought ("T") you would fail the whole course, right?

Your child: Yeah, I really blew that test. I can't believe it! I know I'm going to fail.

You: Okay, so let's talk about the "O" part. Are you 100% sure you will fail the whole course? What is the worst thing that can happen when you do poorly on just one test? Be honest.

Your child: Well, I might fail … I don't know. Plus, there are lots of quizzes and tests this semester in that course. Plus a ton of homework and other assignments!

> *You*:   Right, so ...
> *Your child*:   So I guess doing bad on one test won't kill me. But I can't keep doing bad!
> *You*:   Right, that's true, and we'll work on that. I'll help you. But you understand that one bad grade doesn't mean you'll fail the whole semester?
> *Your child*:   Yeah, I guess I got carried away [then praise ("P") the new thoughts].

Another type of negative thought occurs when teenagers assume they will be embarrassed and that the embarrassment will be horrible. Older children and adolescents worry a lot about being embarrassed. For example, they may give an oral presentation and feel bad when tripping up their words. *The important thing to remember about embarrassment is that it is temporary and manageable!* Be sure to tell your child that everyone gets embarrassed (give some personal examples), that embarrassment does not usually last long, and that your child can handle the embarrassment. Use Worksheet 6.1, the STOP method, and questions outlined above:

> *You*:   Okay, you wrote down that your "S" was giving your oral report and that you thought ("T") you couldn't believe you were embarrassed, right?
> *Your child*:   Yeah, I kept tripping over my words and felt so stupid. I was *so* embarrassed!
> *You*:   Yeah, I can understand that. But let's think about the "O" part. You know, everyone gets embarrassed from time to time. Remember that time I fell off the boat and into the lake with all my clothes on at the family reunion?
> *Your child*:   (Laughing). Yeah, who could forget that!
> *You*:   I felt pretty embarrassed, so everybody gets embarrassed. Have you ever been embarrassed before?
> *Your child*:   Well, yeah, remember the time I fell off the stage during the church play?
> *You*:   Yep. And what did you do?
> *Your child*:   I just got back on stage and kept going, but I felt terrible.
> *You*:   How long did you feel terrible?
> *Your child*:   A couple of hours I guess.
> *You*:   Right, you felt embarrassed but it went away and you were able to handle it, right?
> *Your child*:   Yeah, I guess so.

You: So …

Your child: So I guess feeling embarrassed today will go away too. I already feel better now than I did at school. And I was able to finish my talk.

You: Great job! (the "P" part).

Another type of negative thought that many teenagers have is assuming things are either perfect or terrible, and not in between. For example, a teenager may come home and sulk that her day was awful because of a couple of arguments with her friends. She may ignore, however, the fact that the rest of her day went well. Or a child may be upset because she did not get a perfect grade on a test. If your child has this kind of thought, encourage her to develop more realistic thoughts by thinking about the entire day. Use Worksheet 6.1, the STOP method, and questions outlined above:

You: Okay, you wrote down that your "S" was having a terrible day because of the arguments with your friends and that you thought ("T") the day was terrible, right?

Your child: Yeah, I just feel so rotten about it. I really don't want to go back to school tomorrow.

You: It's okay to feel that way. But let's talk about the "O" part. Was every hour or 100% of the day so terrible?

Your child: Well, no, I got a great grade on my math test and had a lot of fun at lunch with Karen and Justine.

You: Great! It sounds like some of the day went well then.

Your child: Yeah, that's true, most of the day was okay.

You: So what if your day isn't perfect, right? Is any day really perfect, where nothing bad happens?

Your child: Not really. Not in my high school anyway.

You: My day had its ups and downs too. Everyone's does. If a day isn't perfect, then it's a normal day!

Your child: Yeah, I guess that's right [then praise ("P") the new thoughts].

Another type of negative thought many teenagers have is focusing much more on the negative than the positive. For example, teenagers who are nervous about going to class may worry a lot about the questions and comments that others may make about their entrance. In addition, they may ignore the positive things that might happen. If your child has this kind of thought, encourage her to develop more realistic thoughts by thinking about positives as well as negatives. Use Worksheet 6.1, the STOP method, and questions outlined above:

> *You:* Okay, you wrote down that your "S" is having to go to class tomorrow and that you thought ("T") a lot of people are going to bother you with questions, right?
>
> *Your child:* Yeah, everybody's going to ask me where I was this weekend and everything. I just don't want to be bothered! Can't I stay home?
>
> *You:* No, you're going to school tomorrow. Let's talk about the "O" part. What else do you think everyone will say to you?
>
> *Your child:* Some people will be glad to see me. Justin called earlier and said "see you tomorrow!"
>
> *You:* Great! So you might get some looks and stares, and some people might wonder what you did this weekend, but other people will just be happy to see you, right?
>
> *Your child:* Yeah, I think so. And my teachers won't say anything.
>
> *You:* And do you think you'll be bothered with questions all day long?
>
> *Your child:* No, probably just the morning, and I know what I can say.
>
> *You:* Great! (the "P" part).

Another type of negative thought many teenagers have is blaming themselves for things beyond their control. For example, a teenager may blame herself for conflict between two of her friends. If your child has this kind of thought, encourage her to develop more realistic thoughts by thinking about what other explanations are more likely and whether she could really control what happened. Use Worksheet 6.1, the STOP method, and questions outlined above:

> *You:* Okay, you wrote down that your "S" was your two friends fighting and that you thought ("T") you were upset and down on yourself, right?
>
> *Your child:* Yeah, they broke up and won't speak to each other. I feel so bad.
>
> *You:* Why?
>
> *Your child:* Because maybe I could have talked to them more.
>
> *You:* Okay, let's think about the "O" part. Is this really your fault? What else might have caused them to break up?
>
> *Your child:* Well, they're always fighting, and Hector even hung out with another girl!

> *You*:   Those sound like pretty good reasons for a breakup, don't they?
>
> *Your child*:   Yeah, I guess so. But I still feel bad.
>
> *You*:   Yes, it's okay for you to feel bad for your friends, as long as you understand that sometimes people don't get along, and that's not always our fault, right?
>
> *Your child*:   Yeah, that's true. Maybe I can just keep being their friend [then praise ("P") the new thoughts].

Practicing the STOP Method

If your child has many worrisome thoughts about social and performance situations at school, then talk to her *every day* about these thoughts and help her change the thoughts to more realistic ones. In addition, have your child use Worksheet 6.1, practice the STOP method, and draw on the questions listed earlier to take a step back, look at worrisome thoughts, and develop more realistic thoughts. With practice, your child should be able to think more realistically and discover that bad things are not likely to happen and, even if they do, that she is likely to be able to handle whatever does happen. Ask your child as well to practice the relaxation and breathing methods described earlier when challenging her thoughts. In this way, your child is working to manage the physical and thinking parts of her anxiety in social and performance situations.

Do's and Don'ts

Here are a few reminders of do's and don'ts on your part:

Do

- Work with your child to help him breathe well and correctly in social situations.
- Work with your child to help him relax muscle tension in social situations.
- Work with your child to help her manage worrisome thoughts in social situations.

Don't

- Push your child to relax if he feels the methods are not helpful.
- Try methods to manage worrisome thoughts with a young child.
- Work on methods to relax and manage worrisome thoughts without asking your child to practice these methods in real-life situations.

What Is Next?

We have now covered several methods to help your child manage the different parts of his shyness and enhance his social and other skills. With practice, your child should be able to interact with people more and perform before others with less distress. But constant practice is necessary! In the next and final chapter, I discuss ways to help your child maintain the gains he has made. In addition, I cover some special issues that may apply to your child and what you and he can do to address them.

7

Maintaining Gains and Special Issues

Elin is a 9-year-old girl in fourth grade who has made great strides interacting with others at school and making friends. She has always been shy, but her parents and teacher have worked closely with her to encourage her to speak more in class, talk to classmates at lunch and on the playground, and participate in an extracurricular activity. Elin has also made great strides in her social skills. She makes good eye contact and has worked hard to speak more audibly so others can hear her. Elin remains quieter than most children in her class but is certainly more social than before and now has some good friends.

This chapter will cover the following topics:

- Maintaining the gains your child has made.
- Special circumstances regarding your family or your child.
- What to do if you found the methods in this book less helpful.
- Other resources.

Children such as Elin have worked hard to overcome excessive shyness, and hopefully your child has as well. If your child is less shy and interacts better with others, then I am sure that you and he have put in a lot of effort. You might be wondering at this point what you and your child should do next to maintain the gains he has made and ensure that he continues to be effective when speaking to others. This chapter initially presents some suggestions for maintaining the gains you and your child have made. The chapter also covers special circumstances that exist for some children with excessive shyness that may apply to your family or child. I also present suggestions if your child is having some difficulty with the methods in this book. Let's start first with ideas for maintaining what gains your child has made.

Maintaining Gains for Your Child

Many parents are concerned about how to maintain the better social behavior their child developed over time. This is a good concern. We want your child to remain confident and comfortable in social and performance situations, but this will take some ongoing effort. Following are some suggestions for continuing to help your child.

First and foremost, you and your child must continue to practice whatever methods were helpful in getting your child to become more social and more comfortable when speaking to others. A big mistake families make is assuming that once a child shows better social behavior, she is done and everything can go "back to normal." The problem with going "back to normal" is that this might mean going back to allowing a child to avoid certain social situations or speaking for a child or curtailing situations in which a child must speak to others. We do not want this. If you and your child start to back off from using the methods presented in this book, there is a good chance your child will become shyer.

You and your child must practice those methods that you found most successful in helping her be effective in social situations *every day*. This will require great work on your part and on your child's part, but it will be worth the effort. Identify which methods in this book seemed most helpful to your child. Did your child, for example, respond best to everyday practice, independent practice, social skills development, relaxation and breathing work, changing worrisome thoughts, role plays, or some other method we discussed? Every child is different and every child responds to some methods more than they do to others. Concentrate on the method(s) that worked well for your child and *be sure these methods continue to be practiced every day*.

Second, pay close attention to warning signs that might indicate some regression on your child's part. For example, is your child again avoiding more social or performance situations? Does he have physical symptoms of distress when he has to attend some social gathering? Does she start to worry excessively again about what other people are thinking? Think about the different parts of excessive shyness (Chapters 1 and 2) and whether these seem to be recurring for your child. If your child shows these warning signs once in a while, this is not a problem. A child may occasionally ask to miss a soccer practice, for example, but should not do this often. Another child, however, may frequently refuse to attend social gatherings or become quite distressed about interacting with others nearly every day. This child could benefit from greater practice of the methods in this book.

I recommend that you and your child reread this book every so often. Select which chapter or which section of the book seemed most relevant to you and your child and bookmark it. Continue to remain familiar with the methods needed to maintain good social behavior and to manage anxiety. Good practice will help prevent serious problems such as avoidance or distress or worrisome thoughts from developing in the future.

Third, continue to keep track of your child's distress and social behavior every day. Once your child becomes better at speaking and interacting with others, you may be tempted to stop completing the worksheets (Chapter 2) or they may become less of a priority for you. What I have found, however, is that a child who once had trouble interacting with others will have less problems in the future if parents, teachers, friends, and others close to him continue to monitor his social behavior and give him feedback. A child who knows that you are constantly tracking his distress and avoidance in social situations is less likely to avoid these situations.

Fourth, remain in close contact with relevant school officials throughout the school year. As I have mentioned several times, a good working relationship with school officials is essential for helping a child with her social behavior and for preventing problems in the future. Continue to work with school officials so they can let you know immediately if your child becomes distressed, sad, or avoidant of social or performance situations or if she stops talking to others. Ask school officials to let you know of other, possibly related problems as well, such as academic or testing difficulties or threats from other children. In addition, let relevant school officials know immediately if *you* are having any new problems with your child's social behavior. You may be able to develop a quick plan with your child's teacher, for example, to nip new problems in the bud.

Fifth, talk to your child for at least a few minutes each night to review her day. Do not let worries fester or ignore new social challenges your child is facing. Let your child vent about his school day, help him solve problems he may have had with other children, help him practice the methods in this book, and be supportive. These discussions will boost your child's willingness to share his concerns about social or performance situations as well as his willingness to solve emerging problems. Talk to your child as well about recent successes he had and praise him. Your child may volunteer that he spoke to a new child in class that day and that they played together at recess. This kind of behavior needs a big reward!

Sixth, remind your child of the successes she made over the past weeks or months. When a child reverts toward becoming shyer, it is easy to believe that all the work you and she put in went for naught. Not so! Think about where your child began and where she is now. Do not lose sight of the big picture. Think about which situations your child used to avoid, which physical symptoms of distress she had, and which worrisome thoughts troubled her so much. Discuss with your child how these things changed for the better over time. You may even want to show her recent pictures of her outings with friends and others to remind her of her accomplishments. Praise your child for the successes she has achieved and for the ongoing work she puts forth to maintain her social behavior.

Seventh, downplay minor complaints your child has about attending social gatherings. Your child will likely "test" you at some point by complaining about having to attend some social event, about feeling unwell, or about how everyone hates her at school. Be supportive but do not give these statements much attention. Do not worry about your child doing this (she is not back to "square one"). Instead, simply respond matter-of-factly that she is expected to go to the event, that she is fine, and that she should think more realistically about who likes and does not like her at school. Your child may also test you by asking you to order food for her, by throwing a tantrum to avoid a Scout meeting, or by crying to make you feel guilty about volunteering her for the church picnic committee. Be supportive but remain firm in your expectation that your child must practice her social behaviors. Your child will eventually realize that she cannot force you to give in to her poor behavior and her complaints will decrease.

Finally, do not allow backsliding. Once your child has demonstrated certain improvements in her social behavior, you should expect these improvements to be maintained. For example, if your child used to avoid ballet lessons but was able to overcome her excessive shyness and attend these lessons, then regular attendance should continue to be expected. Do not allow backsliding toward greater avoidance. Expect your child to show good social behavior every day. Only extraordinary events such as poor weather or illness should prevent your child from participating in social activities he normally attends. Always nudge your child toward better interactions, better speaking, better social skills, better anxiety control, and better effort.

Special Circumstances Regarding Your Child

I fully appreciate that your family or your child may have special circumstances that serve as a challenge to the methods in this book. Let's talk about those circumstances that I have encountered most over the years and some suggestions for addressing these.

Children with Developmental Disorders

Some children have developmental disorders that affect their ability to interact well with others. Examples include autism, mental retardation, and Asperger's disorder. Autism is a severe developmental disorder that involves delays in social, language, and intellectual ability. Children with autism tend to show little social behavior toward others. They often avoid eye contact, prefer to be by themselves, and show odd behaviors such as frequent twirling or aggression toward themselves or others. If your child has autism, the methods in this book will not likely be helpful. I suggest working closely with qualified mental health professionals who specialize in behavior modification and other intensive strategies to boost social behavior.

Children with mental retardation have intellectual deficits that may be mild, moderate, or severe. Most children with mental retardation, however, especially those with milder forms of the disorder, are usually quite social with others. If your child has mild mental retardation, some of the methods in this book may or may not be helpful. A child with mild mental retardation can benefit from practice and feedback in social situations but may respond less well to the thinking strategies in Chapter 6. If your child has moderate or severe mental retardation, then I suggest working closely with qualified mental health professionals who specialize in behavior modification and other intensive strategies to boost social behavior.

Children with Asperger's disorder often have good intellectual ability but may show odd social behaviors. Some of these children have difficulty starting or maintaining conversations, understanding others' emotions or facial expressions, making eye contact, and using voice inflections to communicate. Other children with Asperger's disorder insist on one-sided conversations, interrupt others frequently, stay focused on only one topic during a conversation, show little empathy for others, and interpret words literally instead of figuratively. If your child has Asperger's disorder, some of the methods in this book can be helpful. I have worked with children with Asperger's disorder to help them interact more seamlessly with others and better understand the emotions and perspectives of others. You may find the methods in this book helpful, but I urge you to consult closely with your child's teacher and other school officials as well as a qualified mental health professional.

If your child has a developmental disorder and you wish to boost his social behavior, then work closely with school officials to design a 504 or individualized education plan that includes methods for improving his interactions with others, such as the methods in this book. Recognize as well that the pace at which your child improves his social behavior may be slower than other children, but that is fine. Your child may need considerable practice regarding the methods presented in this book or may need to concentrate on one method at a time, such as relaxation training. Work closely with school officials as well to ensure that your child's social behavior plan is linked to strong rewards, resolution of new problems or threats that may occur at school, and academic enhancement.

Children with Communication Disorders

Some children also show communication disorders that can affect their ability to understand and produce language and thus interact with others. Children may have the following:

- *Expressive language disorder*, meaning they have limited vocabulary, omit sentence structures, and have trouble recalling words, producing lengthy or complex sentences, using the correct tense, or demonstrating fluency.
- *Mixed receptive-expressive language disorder*, meaning they have expressiveness problems in addition to comprehension deficits such as confusion when spoken to, difficulty understanding words or

sentences, trouble with auditory processing, inattentiveness, and withdrawal.

- *Phonological disorder*, meaning they display errors in sound production, use, or organization, omit sounds such as final consonants in a word, lisp, form words poorly, mix sounds, or have poor articulation.
- *Stuttering*, meaning they frequently repeat or prolong sounds or monosyllablic words, use many interjections or broken words, pause often in speech, avoid certain difficult words, and show great physical tension when speaking.

If your child has a communication disorder, then the methods in this book may still be helpful. However, you will have to work closely with a school speech pathologist or speech therapist who can help your child form words, understand what others are saying, or improve vocabulary. Many interventions for speech-related problems fit well with the methods in this book. For example, children who are taught to improve articulation and receptive language ability need to practice conversing with others. Similarly, children with stuttering often benefit from the relaxation methods detailed in Chapter 6.

Children with Depression

Some children have difficulty interacting with others because they are depressed. Depression involves sad mood, loss of interest or pleasure in activities a child used to enjoy, weight loss, change in appetite, sleep, or activity level, fatigue, feelings of worthlessness, difficulty concentrating, and/or thoughts of death or suicide. Children may be depressed for different reasons, but depression generally leads to fewer interactions with others. Some children who appear to be overly shy actually have symptoms of depression that affect their desire to associate with others.

If you think your child may be depressed, then seek assessment and treatment services from a qualified mental health professional (Chapter 1). Treatments for depression overlap to some extent with the methods in this book, especially becoming more socially active and thinking more realistically. But the methods in this book are not specifically designed to address depression, so be sure to seek professional help. In some cases, a child's shyness could lead to depression, as in the case of a child who rarely interacts with others and is then rejected by others. A qualified mental health professional will be able to determine what kind of depression, if any, your child is experiencing and whether methods related to improving social interaction will be helpful.

Children Who Have Experienced Trauma

Some children also have difficulty interacting with others because they have experienced a recent trauma. Traumas are often highly fearful events such as severe injury, a car accident, a natural disaster, or physical or sexual abuse. Children who experience traumas sometimes withdraw from others and have odd play behaviors, nightmares, and physical symptoms of distress. Other children have not experienced a highly fearful trauma but have experienced a dramatic change in their life that causes them to withdraw from others. Children may be experiencing parental divorce, family conflict at home, loss of a pet, or move to a new school, for example. The methods in this book may be useful to some degree for children who have experienced trauma and recent changes in their lives, but intervention for these children must often focus first on their ability to cope with the trauma. If your child has experienced recent trauma, then I recommend consultation with a qualified mental health professional.

Multiple Children with Excessive Shyness

I mentioned in Chapter 2 that shyness is a trait that often runs in families, meaning shy children often have shy parents. This also means that multiple children in a family may be excessively shy. If you have more than one child who is overly shy, then the methods in this book can be helpful but may need some tweaks. For example, your children could practice speaking to one another effectively before independent practice (Chapters 3 and 4), practice social skills together (Chapter 5), or help each other relax and manage worrisome thoughts (Chapter 6). You may find that one child progresses a little more quickly than another child, so be sure a child is not pressured to keep up or that you do not push too hard.

You may also find it helpful to devote most of your limited time to the child who seems most shy. If the shyest child is older than the others, then concentrating on him will serve as a good model for the others. If the shyest child is younger than the others, then encourage the older siblings to help you practice the methods in this book such as designing a hierarchy, practicing in community situations, and prompting social skills such as eye contact. The greater the involvement of family members (including parents, but also other relatives, friends, or school officials) with the methods in this book, the better the outcome for a shy child.

Perfectionism

Some children who are overly shy also tend to be perfectionists, meaning they have a strong need to perform tasks flawlessly, worry excessively about making mistakes, doubt their ability to achieve goals, and emphasize order and neatness. Perfectionism is not a bad thing unless the behavior interferes with a child's daily functioning. Perfectionism at school can be good in terms of motivating a student to study, for example, but can be bad when the student refuses to attend school or will not hand in homework because of possible mistakes. Shy children sometimes believe that others expect them to be perfect and may withdraw for fear of appearing foolish or making a mistake.

If your overly shy child has aspects of perfectionism, consider whether these characteristics are helpful or not for her. If you feel her perfectionism interferes with her school work, attendance, or interactions with others, then some of the thinking methods in Chapter 6 may be helpful. Children with perfectionism sometimes believe that mistakes carry severe, negative consequences, when actually this is not true. A child may believe that if she does not recite her oral presentation perfectly or say something perfectly, that she will fail or be ridiculed. Ask your child to deliberately make a mistake in different situations and then ask her if the consequences she feared actually happened (be sure they do not). In addition, ask your child to consider one of the questions mentioned in Chapter 6: *So what if I'm not perfect in this situation?* Help your child realize that imperfection is the norm in life and that mistakes are expected and usually tolerated well by others. Most importantly, do not allow your child's perfectionism to serve as an excuse for avoiding interactions with others.

Teasing and Bullying

Many overly shy children are especially sensitive to teasing from others and sometimes withdraw from people out of fear of being teased. Mild teasing is common among children but some shy children respond to teasing in inappropriate ways because they do not know what to do.

Shy children sometimes choose the worst possible options such as crying, remaining alone, or serving as vulnerable targets of future teasing.

The best responses to teasing are to tease back, laugh it off, or change the subject, but many overly shy children have trouble doing this. Instead, encourage your child to simply ignore teasing and walk away. This may seem like avoiding a social situation but the goal is to eliminate rewards that teasers get for their behavior, such as attention and upsetting reactions. Ask your child not to respond to provocation. If teasing is persistent, ask your child to go to a relatively safe area. Most teasing and bullying occur in isolated situations, so tell your child to go to areas of the school where many other children and adults are present.

If this does not work or the teasing/bullying is particularly severe, have your child report the activity to a school counselor or another adult who can help. Consult with school officials to see what can be done to reduce excessive teasing. And, most importantly, tell your child that not all children are teasers and that she must continue to seek people who will be nice to her and become her friend. As your child develops more friendships, teasing is less likely to occur as well because your child will be in the company of others.

Medication

Parents sometimes ask if medication would be helpful for their overly shy or socially anxious child. Some studies indicate that antidepressant medication is helpful for youths with intense social anxiety, although much more testing remains necessary. Medication for youths with social anxiety may be best reserved for adolescents, those with severe symptoms, those with social anxiety *and* depression, and those also receiving therapy from a qualified mental health professional. If you believe that your child could benefit from medication for his social anxiety, then consult a psychiatrist and a clinical psychologist who can conduct a thorough assessment and help you determine an appropriate course of action.

If the Methods in This Book Were Less Helpful for You

I hope you found the methods in this book to be helpful, but what if problems seem to be lingering? Some parents say, for example, that their child speaks a little better to others but still seems nervous or upset or has trouble making friends. Other parents say their child goes to more social functions but still worries constantly about what others are thinking. Still other parents say that nothing seems to have worked. What now?

A few things might be happening. *First, the methods in this book have not been tried long enough.* I know it takes a lot of patience and persistence, but excessive shyness and selective mutism sometimes need to be addressed for at least a few weeks or months before significant results are seen. In addition, the longer a child has been having problems interacting with others, the longer it usually takes for him to become more social. If a shyness or mutism problem has been developing for some time, it will take some time to fix. So, if you have been using the methods in this book for only a short time, I encourage you to keep going. Also, meet with school officials to set up a timeline for these methods. For example, you and they may agree to try certain methods for 3 weeks and then evaluate whether they are working. If not, then the methods could be "tweaked" a bit or some new strategy could be tried.

Second, the methods in this book are not being used consistently. This is the most likely problem. Parents sometimes fall into the trap of using the methods in this book on "bad" days and not on "good" days. Many parents use the methods when a child refuses to attend a social function or will not speak to someone but fail to do so every day. Even if your child has nothing scheduled that day, you can have him practice his social behavior at home (Chapter 3) and work to build his social skills (Chapter 5). You can discuss with your child the thoughts she has in social situations or develop her ability to relax (Chapter 6). You do not want to fall into the habit of working with your child only when there is a problem. In addition, if you do not make the methods in this book a priority, neither will your child. You want to establish a family expectation that social behavior is valued and that your child must practice his social skills often.

Third, some other problem is occurring that prevents the methods in this book from being fully effective. Something unusual may have happened while you were trying to help your child be more social. Examples of unusual events include the birth of a new baby, an illness in the family, a car accident, a job loss, a sudden move to a new area, or some other special event that may have caused some distress. If this is the case, think about whether you are truly ready to put forth the effort needed to help your child speak well to others. If you believe you can, then see how you can "work around" major events to still accomplish what you want to accomplish. If Mom is in the hospital, for example, can other people bring a child to his extracurricular activities?

Fourth, this book may not be completely right for your situation. In Chapter 1 and in other chapters, I outlined different situations that might make this book less helpful. Examples include school refusal behavior, severe behavior problems, intense avoidance of many social situations, school-based threats, and family troubles. If you find that you cannot use the methods in this book because one or more of these or other situations are interfering, then you may wish to consult a qualified mental health professional (Chapter 1). A qualified mental health professional can help you address severe problems that are happening within your child or family. In some cases, excessive shyness or selective mutism is simply one part of these severe problems. A qualified mental health professional can help you deal with all of these problems at once because he or she will know the unique issues that you are facing.

Final Comments and Other Resources

Thank you for reading this book! I appreciate the fact that you are willing to make the effort to help your child become more confident and comfortable in social and performance situations. I hope you find my recommendations helpful now and in the future. If you find that your child's excessive shyness has some special circumstance that I did not cover in this book, please let me know. Most of all, remember that you are not alone. Many parents face what you are facing and many professionals such as I study this problem. Together we can make a difference!

The methods in this book are based on scientific research and my extensive experience working with children with excessive shyness and selective mutism. Although it is not necessary to read the technical information behind the methods covered in this book, some people like to read additional material to find out more about the nature, cause, assessment, and treatment of excessive shyness and selective mutism in children. The bibliography that follows contains a sample of books, book chapters, and journal articles that I and others have written about these youths and that you may find interesting and helpful.

Bibliography

Albano, A. M., Mallick, R., Tourian, K., Zhang, H. F., & Kearney, C. A. (2004). Children and adolescents with social anxiety disorder: School refusal and improvement with venlafaxine ER relative to placebo. *European Neuropsychopharmacology, 14*(Suppl 3), S307–S308.

Chavira, D. A., Stein, M. B., & Malcarne, V. L. (2002). Scrutinizing the relationship between shyness and social phobia. *Journal of Anxiety Disorders, 16*, 585–598.

Cohen, S. L., Chavira, D. A., Shipon-Blum, E., Hitchcock, C., Roesch, S. C., & Stein, M. B. (2008). Refining the classification of children with selective mutism: A latent profile analysis. *Journal of Clinical Child and Adolescent Psychology, 37*, 770–784.

Coplan, R. J., & Arbeau, K. A. (2008). The stresses of a brave new world: Shyness and adjustment in kindergarten. *Journal of Research in Childhood Education, 22*, 377–389.

Coplan, R. J., Arbeau, K. A., & Armer, M. (2008). Don't fret, be supportive! Maternal characteristics linking child shyness to psychosocial and school adjustment in kindergarten. *Journal of Abnormal Child Psychology, 36*, 359–371.

Coplan, R. J., & Armer, M. (2005). 'Talking yourself out of being shy': Shyness, expressive vocabulary, and adjustment in preschool. *Merrill-Palmer Quarterly, 51*, 20–41.

Crozier, W. R., & Hostettler, K. (2003). The influence of shyness on children's test performance. *British Journal of Educational Psychology, 73*, 317–328.

Denissen, J. J. A., Asendorpf, J. B., & van Aken, M. A. G. (2008). Childhood personality predicts long-term trajectories of shyness and aggressiveness in the context of demographic transitions in emerging adulthood. *Journal of Personality, 76*, 67–100.

Greco, L. A., & Morris, T. L. (2001). Treating childhood shyness and related behavior: Empirically investigated approaches used to promote positive social interactions. *Clinical Child and Family Psychology Review, 4*, 299–318.

Heiser, N. A., Turner, S. M., & Beidel, D. C. (2002). Shyness: Relationship to social phobia and other psychiatric disorders. *Behaviour Research and Therapy, 41*, 209–221.

Kearney, C. A. (2005). *Social anxiety and social phobia in youth: Characteristics, assessment, and psychological treatment.* New York: Springer.

Kearney, C. A. (2007). *Getting your child to say "yes" to school: A guide for parents of youth with school refusal behavior.* New York: Oxford University Press.

Kearney, C. A. (2010). *Casebook in child behavior disorders* (4th ed.). Belmont, CA: Wadsworth/Cengage Learning.

Kearney, C. A. (2010). *Helping youths with selective mutism and reluctance to speak: A guide for school-based professionals.* New York: Oxford University Press.

Kearney, C. A., & Albano, A. M. (2007). *When children refuse school: A cognitive-behavioral therapy approach/Parent workbook* (2nd ed.). New York: Oxford University Press.

Kearney, C. A., & Drake, K. (2002). Social phobia. In M. Hersen (Ed.), *Clinical behavior therapy: Adults and children* (pp. 326–344). New York: Wiley.

Kearney, C. A., & Vecchio, J. (2006). Functional analysis and treatment of selective mutism in children. *Journal of Speech and Language Pathology–Applied Behavior Analysis, 1*, 141–148.

Kearney, C. A., & Vecchio, J. L. (2007). When a child won't speak. *Journal of Family Practice, 56*, 917–921.

Ollendick, T. H., & Cerny, J. A. (1981). *Clinical behavior therapy with children.* New York: Plenum (now Springer).

Rubin, K. H., Coplan, R. J., & Bowker, J. C. (2009). Social withdrawal in childhood. *Annual Review of Psychology, 60*, 141–171.

Silverman, W. K., & Kurtines, W. M. (1996). *Anxiety and phobic disorders: A pragmatic approach.* New York: Plenum (now Springer).

Spooner, A., Evans, M. A., & Santos, R. (2005). Hidden shyness in children: Discrepancies between self-perceptions and the perceptions of parents and teachers. *Merrill-Palmer Quarterly, 51*, 437–493.

Vecchio, J. L., & Kearney, C. A. (2005). Selective mutism in children: Comparison to youths with and without anxiety disorders. *Journal of Psychopathology and Behavioral Assessment, 27*, 31–37.

Vecchio, J., & Kearney, C. A. (2009). Treating youths with selective mutism with an alternating design of exposure-based practice and contingency management. *Behavior Therapy, 40*, 380–392.

Viana, A. G., Beidel, D. C., & Rabian, B. (2009). Selective mutism: A review and integration of the last 15 years. *Clinical Psychology Review, 29*, 57–67.